Proinsias Mac Aonghusa

Proinsias Mac Aonghusa is a writer and broadcaster and a political commentator. He is the author of the history of Conradh na Gaeilge/ The Gaelic League, *Ar Son na Gaeilge*, and of various other books both in Irish and English. He was president of *Conradh na Gaeilge,* Chairman of *Bord na Gaeilge,* U.N. representative in South Central Africa in connection with the liberation of Namibia, a member of the Presidential Committee of the World Peace Council, and is the longest serving member of *An Chomhairle Ealaíon*, the Arts Council of Ireland. Throughout his life Mr. Mac Aonghusa has been involved in struggles for civil rights and related activities in Ireland and elsewhere. He is marri   C   rine McGuinness, Chairperson of the Forum for Peac   ; they have one daughter Catríona and two sons   onal and Diarmaid.

What Connolly Said

What Connolly Said

James Connolly's Writings

Selected and Introduced by
Proinsias Mac Aonghusa

N E W
ISLAND
BOOKS

Dublin

What Connolly Said

is first published in 1995 by
New Island Books
2, Brookside,
Dundrum Road,
Dublin 14,
Ireland

ISBN 1 874597 11 1

Cover Design by Jon Berkeley,
Typesetting by Graphic Resources,
Printed in Ireland by Colour Books, Ltd.

Contents

In Memory of two Irish Socialists

Jim Connell 1852 - 1929
author of **The Red Flag**
and
Jim Gralton 1886 - 1945
Republican Revolutionary

Introduction

James Connolly 1868 - 1916

That socialism is an extension of democracy and human freedom was clear to James Connolly, the military commander of the Easter Rising of 1916 in Dublin. So was the fact that the abolition of capitalism is essential if the great mass of people in all parts of the world are to be emancipated.

Now, some eight decades after Connolly's execution by a British firing squad in Dublin, more people are exploited by international capitalism than during his lifetime. Mass unemployment is accepted as an everlasting fact of life in both the developed and undeveloped worlds. The mass media, mainly owned and directed by international monopoly capitalism, are propagandists for the market economy, hostile to trade unionism and inimical to socialism. Capitalism is accepted, either reluctantly or enthusiastically, by most major political groups in Europe, North America, Australasia and in many parts of Asia, and even in Africa. It is cruelly imposed on peoples in Latin America.

But that does not in any way invalidate James Connolly's social, economic and political thinking. Connolly's thinking is as relevant now to a new generation of his countrymen as it ever was. He played a leading part in working class politics in Scotland, the United States and Ireland; his aims were to win decent conditions of employment for all workers, to break the capitalist system by all possible means, and to create a workers' democracy in all countries. He advocated the brotherhood of man, a concept ridiculed by as many in his day as in the closing years of the century.

The grim fact that what passed for socialism in the Soviet Union from the 1920s until the late 1980s, and in parts of central and eastern Europe after the second World War, and then disintegrated is, of course, used as an argument against the ideas and ideals of Connolly and others and in favour of capitalism, or the market economy as it is increasingly called.

But Stalinism is not socialism; dictatorship is not democracy. Socialism as envisaged by Connolly is a liberating force; Stalinism as practised in so many countries for decades was an institutional denial of human rights, a despotism posing as socialism and sometimes as communism.

The peoples of central and eastern Europe had Stalinism imposed upon them following the collapse of German Nazism and Italian Fascism. They did not themselves especially opt for it nor, indeed, for fascism either; they were seldom consulted about their future.

Yet it is not without interest that having tasted capitalism and the realities of the market economy, the peoples of Hungary, Ukraine, Poland and Lithuania have now freely voted for socialist parties and that socialism without Stalinism is now the majority political philosophy in these nations.

Aspects of socialism evolved democratically in Scandinavian countries and the sort of society envisaged by James Connolly became a reality in Norway, Sweden and Denmark. These countries now enjoy high standards of living and are generally regarded as being among the best governed and administered states in the world. Democracy flourished and expanded in Scandinavia along with socialism. Socialism there was a natural and native growth; there was no imposition, no dictatorship, no loss of human rights.

James Connolly was an internationalist. He also was an Irish nationalist, separatist and republican whose views on the invasion and occupation of Ireland were summed up in one sentence of his address to the Court Martial held at his bedside in Dublin Castle on 9 May 1916:

> "Believing that the British Government has no right in Ireland, never had any right in Ireland, and never can have any right in Ireland, the presence in any one generation of Irishmen of even a respectable minority ready to die to affirm that truth makes that Government for ever a usurpation and a crime against human progress."

It might be said that he lived for socialism and died for Ireland. There was no contradiction in this: for Connolly the cause of Ireland was the cause of Labour and the cause of Labour the cause of Ireland. As he pointed out on more than one occasion, the most loyal and committed Irish patriot was the strongest Irish socialist. That the rich would always betray the poor was as obvious to James Connolly, an historian as well as a revolutionary, as it was to Henry Joy McCracken a century before him. It was Connolly who founded the Irish Socialist Republican Party, the first republican and the first socialist party in Ireland. He believed that socialism could not be established in Ireland unless the country were free from foreign domination, and he equally believed that a non-socialist Ireland, even with its green flag and its soldiers in green uniforms and its Parliament on College Green, would still be essentially controlled by London. Capitalism to Connolly was a greater burden on the plain people of Ireland than foreign rule, but both were oppressive. He saw the need for two revolutions, one to overthrow foreign occupation and the other to create a socialist state.

His call to the Irish Citizen Army just days before the Easter Rising is hardly a democratic statement: "In the event of victory hold on to your rifles as those with whom we are fighting may stop before our goal is reached. We are out for economic as well as political liberty. Hold on to your rifles." But it was made in the middle of one of the bloodiest wars fought up to then and at a time when many accepted that the ends justified the means. James Connolly feared a sell-out by some of his nationalist allies. In the event, most members of the Irish Volunteers, confused by contradictory orders, did not rise out against the occupation forces in 1916. In addition, the state ultimately established in 1923 following the War of Independence and a Civil War was a deeply conservative institution where radical ideas or anything approaching socialism were suspect. However, the soldiers wore green uniforms.

Connolly's commitment to socialism is unquestionable. What we cannot know is whether, in reality, he would be prepared to take up arms against fellow nationalists to impose a certain type of philosophy on a politically free Ireland, for that would certainly contradict his life-long democratic approach to public affairs.

James Connolly was born and reared outside Ireland although he was, of course, of Irish parentage. His father, John Connolly, a native Irish speaker from somewhere in Ireland, possibly County Monaghan, who was a manure carter with Edinburgh Corporation, and his mother Mary McGinn, a domestic servant who was born in County Monaghan, were both living in Edinburgh. James was born at 107, Cowgate, Edinburgh on 5 June 1868. The family lived in extreme poverty. That led the eldest son, John, to join the British Army, the second Battalion of the King's Liverpool Regiment, before his 16th birthday. James Connolly joined the Royal Scots Regiment when he was 14 years of age. It was the custom of the day and had no political significance.

He first saw Ireland as a soldier in July 1882 and he served as a British soldier in Ireland until February 1889. That was from the age of 14 to the age of 18, an impressionable period in anyone's life.

Not alone were his parents, and probably their parents also, wretchedly poor but James Connolly himself throughout his whole life, except while in the U.S., was a poor man. He was self educated. He read widely, starting with publications of Michael Davitt's Land League under the influence of an uncle who belonged to the Irish Republican Brotherhood, the Fenians.

He first joined the working class political movement in Dundee in 1889 at the behest of John Leslie, a friend of his brother John and a noted leader of the Social-Democratic Federation. He later became active in the Socialist League, and in Edinburgh, where employed by the Edinburgh Cleansing Department, he helped in recruiting and organising.

Many who joined the Socialist League and the Social-Democratic Federation were Irish, some born in Ireland, others children and grandchildren of Irish immigrants. Some were as concerned with Irish independence as with the emancipation of the working class and they were especially helpful to the Irish Land League. James Connolly was by no means unique in British socialism in regarding the freedom of Ireland as being as important as socialism itself. At the end of the 19th century and the start of the 20th century, the necessity to grant independence to those nations that found themselves involuntary members of the British Empire was a basic belief in British socialist circles. But James Connolly may well have been the most determined of those who appreciated the connection between the two causes.

C. Desmond Greaves's *The Life and Times of James Connolly*, first published by Lawrence and Wishart in London in 1961, is undoubtedly the best study so far of James Connolly and his work in Britain, the US and Ireland. That is not to diminish other works such as Desmond Ryan's *James Connolly*, R.M. Fox's *Connolly the Forerunner* and Proinsias Mac an Bheatha's *Tart na Córa*.

Portrait of a Rebel Father by his daughter Nora Connolly O'Brien, herself a socialist and republican activist, published in Dublin in 1935, is of special interest in presenting Connolly, the family man. The essayist and socialist Robert Lynd, who knew Connolly from 1897 onwards, wrote a fascinating preface for this book. He sums up James Connolly, historian, orator, trade unionist, organiser and republican well. 'In some ways Connolly differed conspicuously from most of the famous Irish patriots both of the past and of his own time. He was a working-class leader and a Nationalist in almost equal proportions. He was at once as patriotic as Garibaldi and as revolutionary as Lenin. The great nation of the poor commanded his loyalty no less than the historic Irish nation that traced its idealism back through the centuries. For him there was nothing paradoxical in this. He saw the cause of the workers and the cause of Ireland not as separate causes but as the same cause,' Lynd wrote. James Connolly wrote a great deal in many papers in Ireland, Scotland, the U.S. and England. These include *Shan Van Vocht, Irish Nation, Workers' Republic, Forward, L'Irlande Libre, Irish Worker, The Harp, The International Socialist Review, The Socialist,* and *The Worker.* Some of these papers were founded and edited by himself.

His *Labour in Irish History,* first published in 1910, is required reading for anyone who wants to understand Ireland and its people. Yet the public in general is but dimly aware of his original, radical and relevant views. That this is so is hardly to the credit of educationalists or to the system of education in any part of Ireland. Is it altogether by accident that James Connolly's works and Patrick Pearse's works are not studied in our schools and colleges? Yet books containing articles, essays and speeches by Connolly and by Pearse are swiftly purchased. But they are seldom reprinted and most of the time Connolly's ideas are not readily available. *The Best of Connolly,* edited by Liam Ó Reágáin and myself nearly three decades ago has long since been out of print.

It may be important that at a time when the commercial mass media are so active and so cleverly hostile both to socialism and to nationalism that James Connolly's thinking should be made available again, especially to younger people. For Connolly's gospel is more likely to supply the foundations for a just society in Ireland than any other.

'Were history what it ought to be, an accurate literary reflex of the times with which it professes to deal, the pages of history would be almost entirely engrossed with a recital of the wrongs and struggles of the labouring people, constituting as they have ever done the vast mass of mankind. But history in general treats the working class as the manipulator of politics treat the working man - that is to say with contempt when he remains passive, and with derision, hatred and misrepresentation whenever he dares evince a desire to throw off the yoke of political or social servitude. Ireland is no exception to this rule. Irish history has ever been written by the master class - in the interests of the master class.'

So wrote James Connolly in the first pages of *Labour in Irish History*.

Even to this day the story of Ireland is told largely from the point of view of the foreign conqueror or of the Irish middle class. Professor J. J. Lee's *Ireland 1912-1985* is one of the few exceptions to this rule.

History is all too seldom told from a working class point of view and it is rarer still for a member of the Irish working class to tell it. The quotations from the writings of James Connolly in this small book all come from the pen and the point of view of the most notable spokesman of the Irish working class.

Proinsias Mac Aonghusa
Dublin, 6th February 1995

What Connolly Said

Socialism and Ireland

If the national movement of our day is not merely to re-enact the old sad tragedies of our past history, it must show itself capable of rising to the exigencies of the moment.

It must demonstrate to the people of Ireland that our nationalism is not merely a morbid idealising of the past, but is also capable of formulating a distinct and definite answer to the problems of the present and a political and economic creed capable of adjustment to the wants of the future.

This concrete political and social ideal will best be supplied, I believe, by the frank acceptance on the part of all earnest nationalists of the Republic as their goal.

Shan Van Vocht, January, 1897

. . . the Republic I would wish our fellow-countrymen to set before them as their ideal should be of such a character that the mere mention of its name would at all times serve as a beacon-light to the oppressed of every land, at all times holding forth promise of freedom and plenteousness as the reward of their efforts on its behalf.

Ibid.

English rule in Ireland is but the symbol of the fact that English conquerors in the past forced upon this country a property system founded upon spoliation, fraud and murder; that, as the present-day exercise of the "rights of property" so originated involves the continual practice of legalised spoliation and fraud, English rule is found to be the most suitable form of government by which the spoliation can be protected, and an English army the most pliant tool with which to execute judicial murder when the fears of the propertied classes demand it.

Ibid.

17

The socialist who would destroy, root and branch, the whole brutally materialistic system of civilisation, which like the English language we have adopted as our own, is, I hold, a far more deadly foe to English rule and tutelage, than the superficial thinker who imagines it possible to reconcile Irish freedom with those insidious but disastrous forms of economic subjection - landlord tyranny, capitalist fraud and unclean usury; baneful fruits of the Norman Conquest, the unholy trinity, of which Strongbow and Diarmuid MacMurchadha - Norman Thief and Irish Traitor - were the fitting precursors and apostles.

Ibid.

If you remove the English army to-morrow and hoist the green flag over Dublin Castle, unless you set about the organisation of the Socialist Republic your efforts would be in vain.

England would still rule you. She would rule you through her capitalists, through her landlords, through her financiers, through the whole array of commercial and individualist institutions she has planted in this country and watered with the tears of our mothers and the blood of our martyrs.

England would still rule you to your ruin, even while your lips offered hypocritical homage at the shrine of that freedom whose cause you had betrayed.

Nationalism without Socialism - without a reorganisation of society on the basis of a broader and more developed form of that common property which underlay the social structure of Ancient Erin - is only national recreancy.

Ibid.

As a Socialist I am prepared to do all one man can do to achieve for our motherland her rightful heritage - independence; but if you ask me to abate one jot or tittle of the claims of social justice, in order to conciliate the privileged classes, then I must decline.

Such action would be neither honourable nor feasible. Let us never forget that he never reaches Heaven who marches thither in the company of the Devil. Let us openly proclaim our faith: the logic of events is with us.

Ibid.

In an independent country the election of a majority of Socialist representatives to the Legislature means the conquest of political power by the revolutionary party, and consequently the mastery of the military and police forces of the State, which would then become the ally of revolution instead of its enemy.

. . . Ireland not being an independent country, the election of a majority of Socialist Republicans would not, unfortunately, place the fruits of our toil so readily within our grasp.

Shan Van Vocht, August , 1897

Socialists are also somewhat divided in their ideas as to what is a proper course in a country like Ireland. One set, observing that those who talk loudest about "Ireland a Nation" are often the most merciless grinders of the faces of the poor, fly off to the extremest limit of hostility to Nationalism and, whilst opposed to oppression at all times, are also opposed to national revolt for national independence.

Another, principally recruited amongst the workers in the towns of North-East Ulster, have been weaned by Socialist ideas and industrial disputes from the leadership of Tory and Orange landlords and capitalists; but as they are offered practical measures of relief from capitalist oppression by the English Independent Labour Party, and offered nothing but a green flag by Irish Nationalism, they naturally go where they imagine relief will come from. Thus their social discontent is lost to the Irish cause. These men see that the workers shot down last winter in Belfast were not shot down in the interests of the Legislative Union - they were shot down in the interests of Irish capitalists. Hence, when a Sinn Feiner waxes eloquent about restoring the Constitution of '82, but remains silent about the increasing industrial despotism of the capitalist; when the Sinn Feiner speaks to men who are fighting against low wages and tells them that the Sinn Fein body has promised lots of Irish labour at low wages to any foreign capitalist who wishes to establish in Ireland, what wonder if they come to believe that a change from Toryism to Sinn Feinism would simply be a change from the devil they do know to the devil they do not know!

Irish Nation, 23rd January, 1909

Let us free Ireland! The profit-grinding capitalists, who robs us of three-fourths of the fruits of our labour, who sucks the very marrow of our bones when we are young, and then throws us out in the street, like a worn-out tool when we are grown prematurely old in his service, is he not an Irishman, and mayhap a patriot, and wherefore should we think harshly of him? Let us free Ireland! "The land that bred and bore us." And the landlord who makes us pay for permission to live upon it. Whoop it up for liberty!

Workers' Republic, 1899

The farmers of Ireland denounced as unpatriotic everything that failed to serve their class interest - including even the labourer's demand for a cottage - let the working class of Ireland follow their lead and test the sincerity of every man's patriotism by his devotion to the interests of labour. In the eyes of the farmers no wagging of green flags could make a land-grabber a patriot; let the workers apply the same test and brand as enemies of Ireland all who believe in the subjection of labour to capital - brand as traitors to his country all who live by skinning Irish labour. For the working class of the world the lesson is also plain. In every country socialism is foreign, is unpatriotic, and will continue so until the working class embracing it as their salvation make socialism the dominant political force...

Workers' Republic, May, 1903

We are trade unionists, but we are more than trade unionists. The trade unionist who is only a trade unionist is to the socialist what the believer in constitutional monarchy is to a republican. The constitutional monarchist wishes to limit the power of the king, but still wishes to have a king; the republican wishes to abolish kingship and puts his trust in the people; the trade unionist wishes to limit the power of the master but still wishes to have masters; the socialist wishes to have done with masters and pins his faith to the collective intelligence of a democratic community.

Workers' Republic, 27th August, 1898

If all the socialists in Ireland who waste their time in cursing the unprogressiveness of the Irish workers, had only sufficient moral courage to declare themselves, they would be astonished at the multitude of their numbers, and would then realise that they were strong enough to ensure respect and toleration. Until they do, we will be compelled to see Irish Tory employers hiding their sweatshops behind orange flags, and Irish home rule landlords using the green sunburst of Erin to cloak their rack-renting in the festering slums of our Irish towns.

Forward, 11th March, 1911

Irish Freedom

It is an inspiration to know the working-class of Ireland in their times of conflict. To see that class resolute, erect, defiant, day by day battling with its Nationalist masters, and in starvation and suffering winning its way to victory, which, at the same time as it closes in grappling with the Irish exploiter, it holds itself uncompromisingly aloof from and hostile to its British rulers and their Irish allies. To know that class is to love it.

And I pity those in whom the narrow prejudices of a colony are still, after 300 years of plantation, too strong to permit them to identify themselves with such a nation.

Forward, 16th August, 1913

Yes, we are a fighting race. Whether it is under the Stars and Stripes or under the Union Jack, planting the flag of America over the walls of Santiago or helping our own oppressors to extend their hated rule over other unfortunate nations, our brave Irish boys are ever to the front.

Workers' Republic, 13th August, 1898

When the Boer has to be robbed of his freedom, the Egyptian has to be hurled back under the heel of his taskmaster, the Zulu to be dynamited in his caves, the Matabele slaughtered beside the ruins of his smoking village, or Afridi to be hunted from his desolated homestead, wheresoever, in short, the bloody standard of the oppressors of Ireland is to be found over some unusually atrocious piece of scoundrelism, look then for the sons of our Emerald Isle, and under the coats of the hired assassin army you will find them.

Ibid.

Whatever we do let us keep on the safe side of the road and not quarrel with the Church - which denounced the United Irishmen and excommunicated the Fenians.

Faith and Fatherland. Oh, yes. But don't forget that when the Englishman was a Catholic and worshipped at the same altar as the Irishman, he plundered, robbed and murdered the Irishman as relentlessly as he did when, with sword in one hand and Bible in the other, he came snuffily chanting his psalms in the train of Oliver Cromwell.

The question of religious faith has precious little bearing upon the question of freedom. Witness Catholic Spain devastating Catholic Cuba, the Catholic capitalists of Italy running down with cannon the unarmed Catholic workmen, the Irish Catholic landlord rack-renting and evicting the Catholic tenant, the wealthy Catholic feasting inside the mansion while the Catholic beggar dies of hunger on the doorstep. And as a companion picture witness the Protestant workmen of Belfast so often out on strike against their Protestant employers and their Protestant ancestors of 100 years ago in active rebellion against the English Protestant Government.

Ibid.

The man whose forefathers manned the walls of Derry is as dear to us as he who traces his descent from the women who stood in the breaches of Limerick. Neither fought for Ireland, but only to decide which English King should rule Ireland. What have we to do with their quarrels? In the words of the United Irishmen - "Let us bury our animosities with the bones of our ancestors."

In the near future when kings and the classes who are makers of kings no longer encumber the earth with their foul presence, how our Irish youth will smile when they read that 200 years ago Irishmen slaughtered each other to decide which English king should have the right to rob the Irish people.

And for that 200 years after the descendents of the respective parties conclusively proved to their own satisfaction that the leader of the other side had been a scoundrel.

And the impartial world looking on examined the evidence and came to the conclusion that on that point, at least, both parties were right. Both kings were scoundrels, ergo the followers of both were - well, never mind.

Ibid.

Every revolutionary effort in Ireland has drawn the bulk of its adherents from the ranks of the disappointed followers of defeated constitutional movements.

Workers' Republic, 22nd July, 1899

As a patriot I hate the class which thrives upon the exploitation of its fellow-countrymen and women, which seizes upon the means of life and withholds them from the poor until their hunger compels them to sell their pittance... I hate this class more than the foreigner. Therefore, I am a Socialist - anxious to purge our national household of its social dishonour.

Workers' Republic, 28th July, 1900

We mean to be free, and in every enemy of tyranny we recognise a brother, wherever be his birthplace; in every enemy of freedom we also recognise our enemy, though he were as Irish as our hills. The whole of Ireland for the people of Ireland - their public property, to be owned and operated as a national heritage, by the labour of free men in a free country.

That is our ideal, and when you ask us what are our methods, we reply: " Those which lie nearest our hands." We do not call for a "United Nation". No nation can be united whilst capitalism and landlordism exist. The system divides society into two warring nations - the robbers and the robbed, the idlers and the workers, the rich and the poor, the men of property and the men of no property. Like Tone and Mitchel before us, we appeal to "that large and respectable class of the community, the men of no property".

Workers' Republic, 5th August, 1899

It may be interesting, then, to place before our readers the Socialist Republican conception of the functions and uses of physical force in a popular movement. We neither exalt it into a principle nor repudiate it as something not to be thought of. Our position towards it is that the use or non-use of force for the realisation of the ideas of progress always has been and always will be determined by the attitude, not of the party of progress, but of the governing class opposed to that party. If the time should arrive when the party of progress finds its way to freedom barred by the stubborn greed of a possessing class entrenched behind the barriers of law and order; if the party of progress has indoctrinated the people at large with the new revolutionary conception of society and is therefore representative of the will of a majority of the nation; if it has exhausted all the peaceful means at its disposal for the purpose of demonstrating to the people and their enemies that the new revolutionary ideas do possess the suffrage of the majority - then, but not till then, the party which represents the revolutionary idea is justified in taking steps to assume the powers of government, and in using the weapons of force to dislodge the usurping class or government in possession, and treating its members and supporters as usurpers and rebels against the constituted authorities always have been treated. In other words, Socialists believe that the question of force is of very minor importance; the really important question is of the principles upon which is based the movement that may or may not need the use of force to realise its object.

Workers' Republic, 22nd July, 1899

We desire to preserve with the English people the same political relations as with the people of France, of Germany or of any other country; the greatest possible friendship, but also the strictest independence. Brothers, but not bedfellows. Thus, inspired by another ideal, conducted by reason not by tradition, following a different course, the Socialist Republican Party of Ireland arrives at the same conclusion as the most irreconcilable Nationalist. The governmental power of England over us must be destroyed; the bonds which bind us to her must be broken.

L'Irlande Libre, 1897

We are told that the English people contributed their help to our enslavement. It is true. It is also true that the Irish people duly contributed soldiers to crush every democratic movement of the English people from the deportation of Irish soldiers to serve the cause of political despotism under Charles I to the days of Featherstone under Asquith. Slaves themselves, the English helped to enslave others; slaves themselves, the Irish people helped to enslave others. There is no room for recrimination.

Irish Worker, 29th November, 1913

Finally, let us say that we are sick of the canting talk of those who tell us that we must not blame the British people for the crime of their rulers against Ireland. We do blame them. In so far as they support the system of society which makes it profitable for one nation to connive at the subjection of another nation they are responsible for every crime committed to maintain that subjection. If there is any section of the British people who believe that Ireland would be justified in ending the British Empire in order to escape from thraldom to it, then that section may hold itself guiltless of any crime against Ireland.

Workers' Republic, 25th March, 1916

When Charles Stewart Parnell was basely deserted in Committee Room 15 by the crowd of adventurers and hack journalists out of whom he had constructed a formidable political party; when he was attacked in Ireland by the tenant farmers who owed much of whatever security they possessed to his skilful leadership; when the priesthood, whom he had elevated to power in the branches of the National League, turned to rend the man under whose firm guidance their influence might have become a power for freedom; when he was, in fact, deserted by the men who had ever been most loud-mouthed in their adulation of his person, it was the leal and true-hearted workingmen of Ireland who sprang to his side and fought his battles. They had never gained, but ever lost by his agitation, but in the supreme crisis of his destinies they rose superior to all other considerations and fought for the man battling against an insulting form of foreign dictation. They asked no reward - and got none. During the early days of the split Mr. Parnell did, indeed, adopt a programme laid before him by Dublin workingmen – a programme embodying nearly every measure advocated as palliative measures by the Socialist parties, but with his untimely death disappeared every hope of seeing that programme adhered to by any Home Rule party.

Workers' Republic, 8th October, 1898

Every succeeding year has seen the Parnellite party become more and more conservative and reactionary. today, in direct opposition to the policy of their great leader, we find the Parnellite chiefs seeking every opportunity to hob-nob with the representatives of Irish land-lordism - hailing their feeblest utterances upon a financial question as the brightest scintillations of wisdom; and not scrupling to tell at Cambridge an audience, composed of the young fledglings of English aristocracy, that the realisation of Ireland's independence was neither possible nor desirable. Followers of Parnell they are indeed, but they follow at such a respectable distance they have lost sight not only of the leader but of his principles.

Ibid.

Brave, heroic, Dublin! Ever battling for the right, ever suffering, ever consecrating by the blood of your children the weary milestones of the path of progress. A year ago the Capitalist class let loose its wolves and slanderers upon you, jailed, batoned and murdered your sons and daughters, but were unable to destroy your holy aspirations for freedom. today the Government of that class once more springs at your throat; once more the blood of your children is shed in the streets, and even some of your misguided children who cheered on that Government in its outrage of a year ago are now ruthlessly slaughtered by that same Government.

Magnificent Dublin! As you emerged with spirit unbroken and heart undaunted from your industrial tribulation, so you will arise mightier and more united from the midst of the military holocaust with which this Government of all the treacheries meets your plans for political freedom.

Forward, 1st August, 1914

Mr. John E. Redmond has just earned the plaudits of all the bitterest enemies of Ireland and slanderers of the Irish race by declaring, in the name of Ireland, that the British Government can now safely withdraw all its garrisons from Ireland, and that the Irish slaves will guarantee to protect the Irish estate of England until their masters come back to take possession - a statement that announces to all the world that Ireland has at last accepted as permanent this status of a British province. Surely no inspiration can be sought from that source.

. Irish Worker, 8th August, 1914

You cannot fight the devil with brimstone; you cannot beat the politicians at their own game. The secret methods of character assassination, elaborated by hordes of ward politicians and perfected by the foul manipulators of Hibernian lodges, cannot be countered by any mere policy of marking time, nor defeated by any organisation that hesitates to attack in the open the organisations that are everywhere in secret striking at our very life.

Let us be plain-spoken! The United Irish League, the Parliamentary Party, the Board of Erin Hibernians have at the present moment a thousand foul agencies at work to destroy the Volunteers who dared to spoil their attempt to betray Ireland into the grasp of British Imperialism. The hatred of these organisations for the men and women who dared to prefer Ireland to the Empire, who dared to prefer the memories of a glorious past and the hopes of a glorious future to the sordid service of England - that hatred is as deep and as implacable as is ever the hatred of the traitor spoiled of the fruits of his treachery.

Irish Worker, 10th October, 1914

The working class has ever refused to be drawn into any mere anti-English feeling; it refuses to be drawn into it now. It has always refused to consider that hatred of England was equivalent to love of Ireland, or that true patriotism required an Irish man or woman to bear enmity to the toiling masses of the English population.

Irish Worker, 31st October, 1914

The Labour Movement in Ireland stands for the ownership of all Ireland by all the Irish; it therefore fights against all things calculated to weaken the hold of the Irish upon Ireland, as it fights for all things calculated to strengthen the grasp of the Irish people upon Ireland and all things Irish... Alone in Ireland the working class has no ties that bind it to the service of the Empire. Hunger and the fear of hunger have driven thousands of our class into the British army; but for whatever pay or pension such have drawn therefrom they have given service, and owe neither gratitude nor allegiance. For those still held to that accursed bargain as reservists, etc., we have no feelings except compassion; the British Shylock will hold them to the bond. Other classes serve England for the sake of dividends, profits, official positions and sinecures - a thousand strings drawing them to England for the one patriotic tie that binds them to Ireland. The Irish working class as a class can only hope to rise with Ireland.

Equally true is it that Ireland cannot rise to Freedom except upon the shoulders of a working class knowing its rights and daring to take them.

Ibid.

Two members of the Fenian organisation - Kelly and Deasy - were trapped in Manchester, and lay awaiting trial in an English prison. The Fenians in that city resolved to rescue them. This they did by stopping the prison van upon the road between Manchester and Salford, breaking open the van, shooting a policeman in the act, and carrying off their comrades under the very eyes of the English authorities. Out of a number of men arrested for complicity in the deed, three were hanged. These three were ALLEN, LARKIN and O'BRIEN - the three

Manchester Martyrs whose memory we honour today. Why do we honour them?

Workers' Republic, 20th November, 1915

We honour them because of their heroic souls. Let us remember that by every test by which parties in Ireland today measure political wisdom, or personal prudence, the act of these men ought to be condemned. They were in a hostile city, surrounded by a hostile population; they were playing into the hands of the Government by bringing all the Fenians out in broad daylight to be spotted and remembered; they were discouraging the Irish people by giving them another failure to record; they had no hopes of foreign help even if their brothers in Ireland took the field spurred by their action; at the most their action would only be an Irish riot in an English city; and finally, they were imperilling the whole organisation for the sake of two men. These were all the sound sensible arguments of the prudent, practical politicians and theoretical revolutionists. But "how beggarly appear words before a defiant deed!"

The Fenians of Manchester rose superior to all the whines about prudence, caution and restraint, and saw only two of their countrymen struck at for loyalty to freedom, and seeing this, struck back at the enemy with blows that are still resounding through the heart of the world. The echo of those blows has for a generation been as a baptismal dedication to the soul and life of thousands of Irish men and women, consecrating them to the service of freedom.

Ibid.

ALLEN, LARKIN and O'BRIEN died that the right of their small nationality to independence might be attested by their blood - died that some day an Irish Republic might live.

Ibid.

Was it wise then, or commendable, for the men of '67 to rebel against the Empire that their and our fathers have helped to build or steal? There are thousands of answers to that question but let the European battle-fields of today provide the one all-sufficient answer.

All these mountains of Irish dead, all these corpses mangled beyond recognition, all these arms, legs, eyes, ears, fingers, toes, hands, all these shivering putrefying bodies and portions of bodies - once warm living and tender parts of Irish men and youths - all these horrors buried in

Flanders or the Gallipoli Peninsula, are all items in the price Ireland pays for being part of the British Empire. All these widows whose husbands were torn from their sides and forced to go to war, their prayers and tears for the ones who will return no more, are another part of the price of the Empire. All those fatherless orphans, who for the last time have heard the cheery laugh of an affectionate father, and who must for years suffer all the bitter hardships of a childhood poorly provided for against want and hunger - all those and their misery are part of the price Ireland pays for Empire. All those shattered, maimed and diseased wrecks of humanity who for years will crowd our poorhouses and asylums, or crawl along our roads and streets affronting our health by their wounds, and our comfort by their appeals for charity - all, all are part of the price Ireland pays for the glory of being an integral part of the British Empire.

Ibid.

We cannot conceive of a free Ireland with a subject working class; we cannot conceive of a subject Ireland with a free working class. But we can conceive of a free Ireland with a working class guaranteed the power of freely and peacefully working out its own salvation.

Workers' Republic, 18th December, 1913

We do not believe that the existence of the British Empire is compatible with either the freedom or security of the Irish working class. That freedom and that security can only come as a result of complete absence of foreign domination. Freedom to control all its own resources is as essential to a community as to an individual. No individual can develop all his powers if he is even partially under the control of another, even if that other sincerely wishes him well. The powers of the individual can only be developed properly when he has to bear the responsibility of all his own actions, to suffer for his mistakes, and to profit by his achievements.

Ibid.

No nation is worthy of independence until it is independent. No nation is fit to be free until it is free. No man can swim until he has entered the water and failed and been half drowned several times in the attempt to swim.

A free Ireland would make dozens of mistakes, and every mistake would cost it dear, and strengthen it for future efforts. But every time it, by virtue of its own strength, remedied a mistake it would take a long step forward towards security. For security can only come to a nation by a knowledge of some power within itself, some difficulty overcome by a strength which no robber can take away.

Ibid.

As the separate individual is to the family, so the separate nation is to humanity. The perfect family is that which best draws out the inner powers of the individual, the most perfect world is that in which the separate existence of nations is held most sacred. There can be no perfect Europe in which Ireland is denied even the least of its national rights; there can be no worthy Ireland whose children brook tamely such denial. If such denial has been accepted by soulless slaves of politicians then it must be repudiated by Irish men and women whose souls are still their own.

The peaceful progress of the future requires the possession by Ireland of all the national rights now denied to her. Only in such possession can the workers of Ireland see stability and security for the fruits of their toil and organisation. A destiny not of our fashioning has chosen this generation as the one called upon for the supreme act of self-sacrifice - to die if need be that our race might live in freedom.

Workers' Republic, 12th February, 1916

Did you ever hear an Irish man or woman say, "my grandfather fought for England in '98" and expect to get popular approval or respect because of that fact? You did not. But if ever you met a man or woman who could say that their grandfather or great grandfather, fought against England in '98, were you not proud to meet them, and did not you and all your friends look upon them with respect because of what their ancestor had done against England? You did. And you were quite right too.

Workers' Republic, 26th February, 1916

But some people in Ireland do honour the men who fought for England in '98 or pretend to honour them. . . Who are they? Why, they are the men who locked us out in 1913, the men who solemnly swore that they would starve three-fourths of the workers of Dublin in order to compel them to give up their civil rights - the right to organise. The recruiters in Dublin and in Ireland generally are the men who pledged themselves together in an unholy alliance to smash trade unionism, by bringing hunger, destitution and misery in fiercest guise into the homes of Dublin's poor.

On every recruiting platform in Dublin you will see the faces of the men who in 1913-14 met together day by day to tell of their plans to murder our women and children by starvation, and are now appealing to the men of those women and children to fight in order to save the precious skins of the gangs that conspired to starve and outrage them.

Who are the recruiters in Dublin? Who is it that sits on every recruiting committee, that spouts for recruits from every recruiting platform?

Who are they? They are the men who set the police upon the unarmed people in O'Connell Street, who filled the jails with our young working class girls, who batoned and imprisoned hundreds of Dublin workers, who racked and pillaged the poor rooms of the poorest of our class, who plied policemen with drink, suborned and hired perjurers to give false evidence, murdered John Byrne and James Nolan and Alice Brady, and in the midst of a Dublin reeking with horror and reeling with suffering and pain publicly gloated over our misery and exulted in their power to get "three square meals per day" for their own overfed stomachs.

These are the recruiters. Every Irish man or boy who joins at their call gives these carrion a fresh victory over the Dublin working class - over the working class of all Ireland.

Ibid.

The United Irishmen waited too long, the Young Irelanders waited too long, the Fenians waited too long. This is the opinion of every student of history worthy of the name. But who dare censure these brave men and women? Assuredly not the men and women of our generation. To us also a great opportunity has come. Have we been wise? The future alone can tell.

Workers' Republic, 11th March, 1916

The national press of Ireland, the true national press, uncorrupted and unterrified, has largely succeeded in turning back the tide of demoralisation, and opening up the minds of the Irish public to a realisation of the truth about the position of their country in the war. The national press of Ireland is a real flag of freedom flying for Ireland despite the enemy, but it is well that also there should fly in Dublin the green flag of this country as a rallying point of our forces and embodiment of all our hopes. Where better could that flag fly than over the unconquered citadel of the Irish working class, Liberty Hall, the fortress of the militant working class of Ireland.

Workers' Republic, 8th April, 1916

We are out for Ireland for the Irish. But who are the Irish? Not the rack-renting, slum-owning landlord; not the sweating, profit-grinding capitalist; not the sleek and oily lawyer; not the prostitute pressman - the hired liars of the enemy. Not these are the Irish upon whom the future depends. Not these, but the Irish working class, the only secure foundation upon which a free nation can be reared.

Ibid.

The cause of labour is the cause of Ireland, the cause of Ireland is the cause of labour. They cannot be dissevered. Ireland seeks freedom. Labour seeks that an Ireland free should be the sole mistress of her own destiny, supreme owner of all material things within and upon her soil. Labour seeks to make the free Irish nation the guardian of the interests of the people of Ireland, and to secure that end would vest in that free Irish nation all property rights as against the claims of the individual, with the end in view that the individual may be enriched by the nation, and not by the spoiling of his fellows.

Ibid.

Irish Language

I believe the Gaelic movement has great promise of life in it, but that promise will only be properly fulfilled when it naturally works its way into the life of the nation, side by side with every other agency making for a regenerated people.

The chief enemy of a Celtic revival today is the crushing force of capitalism which irresistibly destroys all national or racial characteristics, and by sheer stress of its economic preponderance reduces a Galway or a Dublin, a Lithuania or a Warsaw to the level of a mere second-hand imitation of Manchester or Glasgow.

In the words of Karl Marx, "Capitalism creates a world after its own image", and the image of Capitalism is to be found in the industrial centres of Great Britain.

A very filthy image indeed.

Workers' Republic, 1st October, 1898

You cannot teach starving men Gaelic; and the treasury of our national literature will and must remain lost forever to the poor wage-slaves who are contented by our system of society to toil from early morning to late at night for a mere starvation wage.

Ibid.

Therefore, I say to our friends of the Gaelic movement - your proper place is in the ranks of the Socialist Republican Party, fighting for the abolition of this accursed social system which grinds us down in such a manner; which debases the character and lowers the ideals of our people to such a fearful degree, that to the majority of our workers the most priceless manuscript of ancient Celtic lore would hold but a secondary place in their esteem beside a rasher of bacon.

Help us to secure to all our fellow-countrymen, a free, full, and happy life; secure in possession of a rational, human existence, neither brutalised by toil nor debilitated by hunger, and then all the noble characteristics of our race will have full opportunity to expand and develop. And when all that is good in literature, art and science is recognised as the property of all - and not the heritage of the few - your ideals will receive the unquestioned adhesion of all true Irishmen.

Ibid.

Let the great truth be firmly fixed in your mind that the struggle for the conquest of the political state of the capitalist is not the battle, it is only the echo of the battle. The real battle is being fought out, and will be fought out, on the industrial field.

The Harp, April, 1908

Besides, it is well to remember that nations which submit to conquest or races which abandon their language in favour of that of an oppressor do so, not because of the altruistic motives, or because of a love of brotherhood of man, but from a slavish and cringing spirit.

From a spirit which cannot exist side by side with the revolutionary idea.

This was amply evidenced in Ireland by the attitude of the Irish people towards their language.

For six hundred years the English strove to suppress that mark of the distinct character of the Gael - their language, and failed. But in one generation the politicians did what England had failed to do.

The great Daniel O'Connell, the so-called liberator, conducted his meetings entirely in English. When addressing meetings in Connaught, where, in his time, everybody spoke Gaelic and over 75 per cent of the people nothing else but Gaelic, O'Connell spoke exclusively in English. He thus conveyed to the simple people the impression that Gaelic was something to be ashamed of - something fit for only ignorant people. He pursued the same course all over Ireland.

As a result of this and similar actions the simple people turned their backs upon their own language and began to ape "the gentry". It was the beginning of the reign of the toady and the crawler, the *seoinin* and the slave.

Ibid.

It is not ancient history, but the history of yesterday that old Irish men and women would speak Irish to each other in the presence of their children, but if they caught son or daughter using the language the unfortunate child would receive a cuff on the ear accompanied with the adjuration:- "Speak English, you rascal - speak English like a gintleman!"

It is freely stated in Ireland that when the Protestant evangelisers, soupers they call them at home, issued tracts and Bibles in Irish in order to help the work of proselytising, the Catholic priesthood took advantage of the incident to warn their flocks against reading all literature in Gaelic. Thus still further discrediting the language.

Ibid.

We are not bigoted on the language question: we recognise however, that in this country those who drop Irish in favour of English are generally actuated by the meanest of motives, are lick-spittles desirous of aping the gentry, whereas the rank and file of the Gaelic movement are for the most part thoroughly democratic in sentiment and spirit. If these latter did not so persistently revert for their inspiration to the past they would lose nothing and gain much in our estimation.

But as this is neither a political nor an economic question it is outside our province to make any pronouncement upon it. We wish all Socialists to practise the same reserve. In the course of an interpellation in the French Chamber upon the attitude of the French Government towards the Breton language, Mr. Gérault-Richard, editor of *La Petite République*, most aggressively put himself upon record against granting further toleration to that tongue in Brittany. He was uncompromising in his hostility, but on the question of Socialists accepting favours and places (bribes) from capitalist ministries he was pliability itself.

Workers' Republic, March, 1903

International

We are willing to work and co-operate heartily with any one who will aid us in arousing the slumbering giant of labour to a knowledge of its rights and duties.

The Harp, January, 1910

Whilst we are as firm as ever in our belief that the only hope for Ireland, as for the rest of the world, lies in a revolutionary reconstruction of society, and that the working class is the only one historically fitted for that great achievement, we are prepared to co-operate with all who will help forward the industrial and political organisation of labour, even should the aim they set for such organisation be far less ambitious than our own.

Ibid.

Capitalism teaches the people the moral conceptions of cannibalism - the strong devouring the weak; its theory of the world of men and women is that of a glorified pig-trough where the biggest swine gets the most swill. The idea of human relations which would grow out of the working class of Ireland solidifying and concentrating their forces for their common benefit - and their abandonment of the idea behind the English system of trade unions which has hitherto cramped and dwarfed their mind and powers - would make for human brotherhood and a conception of the universe worthy of a really civilised people.

Ibid.

Perhaps some day there will arise in America a socialist writer who in his writing will live up to the spirit of the Communist Manifesto that the socialists are not apart from the labour movement, are not a sect, but are simply that part of the working class which pushes on all others, which most clearly understands the line of march.

The International Socialist Review, February, 1910

We have not any knowledge of any country in which the working class more readily rallies to an appeal to its class feeling than in Ireland. Whilst the knowledge of theoretical socialism is but meagerly distributed amongst the workers, that feeling or knowledge which the socialists call class-consciousness is deep-seated, wide-spread and potent in its influence.

The Harp, April, 1910

Briefly stated, the facts as they are known to us all are that all over the United States the capitalist class is even now busily devising ways and means by which the working class can be disenfranchised. In California it is being done by exacting an enormous sum for the right to place a ticket upon the ballot; in Minnesota the same end is sought by a new primary law; in the south by an educational test to be imposed only upon those who possess no property; in some states by imposing a property qualification upon candidates; and all over by wholesale counting out of socialist ballots, and wholesale counting in of fraudulent votes. In addition to this we have had in Colorado and elsewhere many cases where the hired thugs of the capitalists forcibly occupied the polling booths, drove away the real voters and themselves voted in the name of every citizen on the list.

The International Socialist Review, October, 1909

Socialism in Ireland needs a representative in the press devoted to its cause, and unhampered by any other affiliation. That representative we propose to be. It shall be our aim to place our columns and our poor abilities at the service of all the brave and unselfish men and women who are battling for social righteousness against the forces of iniquity which control and poison human life today.

The Harp, January, 1910

Let us have patience with one another; let us remember the truth that Irishmen are ever ready to forget, *viz.*, that we must tolerate one another or else be compelled to tolerate the common enemy. This does not mean that we have altered or abandoned, or propose to alter or abandon, our belief in the correctness of the principles for which we stood in Ireland from 1896 onward. We still believe that those principles contain the salvation of Ireland, socially and nationally, we still believe that the struggle of Ireland for freedom is a part of the worldwide upward movement of the toilers of the earth, and we still believe that the emancipation of the working class carries within it the end of all tyranny - national, political and social.

Ibid.

I have spent a great portion of my life alternating between interpreting Socialism to the Irish and interpreting the Irish to the Socialists.

Forward, 3rd May, 1913

At least as far as the Socialists of Great Britain are concerned, they always seem to me to exhibit towards the Irish working-class democracy of the Labour movement the same inability to understand their position and to share in their aspirations as the organised British nation, as a whole, has shown to the struggling Irish nation it has so long held in subjection.

Ibid.

The Socialist Party of Ireland recognises and most enthusiastically endorses the principle of internationalism, but it realises that that principle must be sought through the medium of universal brotherhood rather than by self-extinction of distinct nations within the political maw of over-grown Empires.

Forward, 11th March, 1911

My reading of history tells me that in all great social changes the revolutionary class always fails of success until it is able to do the work of the class it seeks to destroy, and to do it more efficiently. And when it has so perfected itself that it is able to perform this work, neither gods nor men can stop its onward march to victory. In other words, a new social order cannot supplant the old until it has its own organisation ready to take its place. Within the social order of capitalism I can see no possibility of building up a new economic organisation fit for the work of superceding the old on socialist lines, except that new order be built upon the lines of the industries that capitalism itself has perfected. Therefore I am heart and soul an industrial unionist. But because I know that the capitalist class is alert and unscrupulous in its use of power, I do not propose to leave it the uncontested use of the powers of the state. And because I realise that human nature is a wonderful thing, that the soul of man gives expression to strange and complex phenomena, and that no man knows what powers or possibilities for good or evil lie in humanity, I try to preserve my receptivity towards all new ideas, my tolerance towards all manifestations of social activity.

Forward, 9th May, 1914

The moment the worker no longer believes in the all-conquering strength of the employer is the moment when the way opens out to the emancipation of our class.

The master class realise this, and hence all their agencies bend their energies towards drugging, stupefying and poisoning the minds of the workers - sowing distrust and fear amongst them.

The ruling class of the British Empire also know it, and hence they also utilise every agency to spread amongst the subject races a belief in the luck of England, in the strength of England, in the omnipotence of England. That belief is worth more to the British Empire than ten army corps; when it goes, when it is lost, there will be an uprising of resurgent nationalities - and a crash of falling Empires.

Should we not therefore admire the Empire that in the face of danger can yet fascinate and enthral the minds of its slaves and keep them in mental as well as physical subjection ... ?

Workers' Republic, 9th October, 1915

The English have acquired somehow the reputation of being blunt, business-like people, with a frank, open nature, whereas the history of their dealings with other people show them to have been the shrewdest masters of the diplomatic game the world has ever seen.

In Ireland, as their own State Papers frankly declare, they employed forgery, bribery, and murder as part of their daily weapons for the subjugation of the country; in India their own chief apologist, Lord Macaulay, records that Lord Clive, the founder of their Indian Empire, forged the name of an Indian patriot to serve the interests of the Empire, and Warren Hastings, when put on trial for extortion, blackmail, bribery, torture, wholesale plunder, invasion and conquest of neutral states, was proven guilty but let off scot free on the ground that he had indulged in those crimes for the good of the Empire.

Workers' Republic, 6th November, 1915

In Europe the same guileless John Bull has assiduously kept stirring the pot of international hatreds and jealousies, pitting nations against nations, and ever fanning the embers of war into consuming flames. Sometimes he supported subject nations against their tyrants, sometimes despots against their struggling subjects, sometimes preached the doctrine of national rights, sometimes (as at the Congress of Vienna, 1815) acted the part of the chief criminal in dividing and parcelling out ancient nations. Ready to fly to arms to defend the rights of neutrals, still more ready to trample roughshod over neutral rights when it served his purpose; ever appealing to God and the Bible, and always convinced that crimes committed by John Bull became virtues, and virtuous acts by his enemies became blasphemous mockeries of the Most High.

Ibid.

The diplomat holds all acts honourable which bring him success, all things are righteous which serve his ends. If cheating is necessary, he will cheat; if lying is useful, he will lie; if bribery helps, he will bribe; if murder serves, he will order murder; if burglary, seduction, arson or forgery brings success nearer, all and each of these will be done.

Ibid.

No revolutionary movement is complete without its poetical expression. If such a movement has caught hold of the imagination of the masses, they will seek a vent in song for the aspirations, the fears and hopes, the loves and hatreds engendered by the struggle. Until the movement is marked by the joyous, defiant, singing of revolutionary songs, it lacks one of most distinctive marks of a popular revolutionary movement; it is a dogma of a few, and not the faith of the multitude.

Songs of Freedom, 1907

The governing classes can declare unconstitutional whatever political movements they do not like. Knowing this, many Irishmen run into secret societies in order to satisfy their hatred of the Constitution. It is against the Constitution to join a republican secret society. But it is also against the Constitution to keep a dog without a licence. The romance which might attach to the former act is cruelly dissipated by the reflection that the law is as remorseless in hunting down the offender in the latter.

Workers' Republic, 9th September, 1898

A great socialist writer, Karl Marx, has said that history repeats itself - once as tragedy, and once as farce. We suppose that the real explanation of the supposed tendency of history to repeat itself lies in the tendency of human beings to imitate whatever action has impressed itself much upon the imagination, just as in a company of individuals we generally find some persons almost unconsciously imitating the mannerisms of any obtrusive personality in the group.

Workers' Republic, 8th January, 1916

Nationalist Party

Mr. Redmond has a record as a reactionist difficult to excel. Long before the Parnell split, he denounced the Irish agricultural labourers in a speech at Rathfarnham, near Dublin, for forming a trade union to protect their own interests. On the granting of Local Government in 1898, a measure that first enfranchised the Irish working class on local bodies, Mr. Redmond made a speech counselling the labourers to elect landlords to represent them - a speech truly characterised by Mr. Michael Davitt in the House of Commons as the "speech of a half-emancipated slave". The labourers in town and country treated Mr. Redmond's advice with contempt and elected men of their own class all over Ireland. Compelled by the imperative necessity of maintaining in power a Home Rule government, Mr. Redmond votes for every measure of social reform the defeat of which would lead to the resignation of said government, but quietly acquiesces in every exemption of Ireland from progressive measures. Mr. Redmond believes that the Irish people are capable of governing their country, but opposed the proposal of Mr. T.W. Russell to allow the Irish people to control their own schools under the Local Government Act of 1898. Mr. Redmond bewails the fact that lack of employment compels the Irish workers to emigrate at the rate 30,000 per year, but opposed the attempt of the Labour party to compel the government to recognise its duty to provide work for them at home; Mr. Redmond believes that all public servants and representatives should be paid for their services to the state from the funds of the state, but is opposed to payment of members being extended to Ireland; Mr. Redmond's heart bleeds for the poor of Ireland, but he would not vote for the Feeding of School Children's Act to be applied to Ireland, and Mr. Redmond is a friend of the Labour Party in England (!), but his party fights to the death against every independent candidature of Labour throughout the purely Nationalist districts of Ireland.

Forward, 18th March, 1911

A real representative of the Irish democracy might go on to show how Mr. Joseph Devlin's organisation, the A.O.H., supposed to be the Ancient Order of Hibernians, but by some believed to be the Ancient Order of Hooligans, has spread like an ulcer throughout Ireland, carrying social and religious terrorism with it into quarters hitherto noted for their broad-mindedness and discernment.

How it has organised the ignorant, the drunken and the rowdy, and thrown the shield of religion around their excesses; how it has made it impossible to conduct a political contest in the South of Ireland except on the lines of civil war; and how every man who dares to oppose the Redmondite party, or every man within that party who opposes the A.O.H., must be at all times prepared to take his life in his hands ...

Every shade of political feeling in Ireland, outside of the official gang at the head of the United Irish League, agrees that this organisation of Mr. Devlin's creation, and of whose work Mr. Redmond accepts the fruits, is the greatest curse yet introduced into the political and social life of Ireland.

Ibid.

Anybody who wants to defend faith and fatherland very badly can get a job up north just now. Carson's army is out on the warpath demanding the blood of the "Papists", and "Wee Joe Devlin" has been lecturing in Belfast upon "Isaac Butt", whilst the organisation of which he is head is organising scabbery in Dublin; faith and fatherland is being attacked from all sides, and the Hibernian attack, under cover of defending the Pope, will be more harmful than the Orangemen who save the Pope under cover of attacking the faith.

Irish Worker, 14th January, 1914

The head of the Ancient Order of Hibernians praising Isaac Butt, a Protestant Home Ruler, is very amusing considering that if Isaac Butt was alive every Hibernian in Ireland would be bound to oppose him even for the humblest position in Ireland. The Catholics of Ireland are the most tolerant people in Ireland - always have been - but the aim of the "Hibs" is to convert this tolerant people into a nation of furious bigots and sectarian patriarchs. They stink in the nostrils of every honest man and woman.

Ibid.

The Municipal Elections in Dublin never fail to provide mirth for the multitude. The fun has already begun in Merchants' Quay Ward, where Andrew Breslan, a working carpenter and nominee of the Dublin Labour Party, is being opposed by Mr. John Scully, High Sheriff of Dublin City. Scully is running in the interests of the United Irish League and high rents, slum tenements, rotten stair-cases, stinking-yards, high death rates, low wages, Corporation jobbery and margarine wrapped up in butter paper.

Also several other things. Mr. Scully is a provision merchant: as such he is bound to furnish provisions upon the demand of his customers, and as High Sheriff he is bound to provide hangmen upon the demand of the British Government; or be a hangman himself if the supply of professional hangmen failed. If Robert Emmet was to be hanged tomorrow, and the professional hangman went on strike, Mr. Scully is bound by his oath of office to do the job and hang the patriot.

Ibid.

...the Home Rule press is but a sewer-pipe for the pouring of English filth upon the shores of Ireland.

Irish Worker, 12th September, 1914

As I think of the hundreds of good men I have known, fathers of families, husbands, sons with aged parents, etc., who have been enticed to leave their homes and dear ones and march out to battle for an empire that never kept faith with the Irish race, and think that it was Wee Joe's influence that led them to their folly, I think things that the Defence of the Realm Acts will not permit me to print.

Belfast opponents of Joe Devlin usually refer to him sarcastically as the "Wee Bottlewasher", alluding to his position before he climbed into power. The sarcasm is pointless. A bottlewasher was an honest occupation, but a recruiting sergeant luring to their death the men who trusted him and voted him into power is - ah well, let us remember the Defence of the Realm Act.

Workers' Republic, 28th August, 1915

The present writer cannot ride up the Falls Road in his own motor car, the penny tram has to do him. But thank God, there are no fresh made graves in Flanders or the Dardanelles filled by the mangled corpses of men whom he coaxed or bullied into leaving their homes and families.

And that consolation counts more to the peace of his soul than would the possession of a motor car, or the companionship of grossly overfed boon companions of the bottlewasher - or the bottle.

There are widows in Belfast today whose husbands would still be with them if they had taken my advice; there are orphans in Belfast today whose fathers would still be able to work for them if they had taken my advice; there are stricken mothers and fathers in Belfast today whose sons would still be smiling and happy at the family hearth today if my advice had been listened to. And I am confident that it will not be long before these widows, orphans and bereaved parents with every sob and sigh will breathe a curse upon the conscienceless politician to whose advice they did listen.

Ibid.

Without the invigorating presence of an alert and independent labour party in its midst the Irish House of Commons will be for years a most reactionary and anti-democratic assembly, setting a bad example to Tories and reactionists everywhere. It will be obsessed with the idea of placating the reactionary elements in Ulster, and thus justifying itself against their aspersions. What this means you can best understand when you realise that Ulster is the most capitalist part of Ireland, that the game will be to represent every bit of labour legislation which menaces capitalist profits as an attack upon the industries of Ulster, and that the fear of this cry will cause the new Irish Government, and every non-labour element in Parliament, to oppose all social legislation. Only a strong and determined labour group, with a true revolutionary outlook, will be able to withstand this cry, force forward progressive legislation and combat reactionary measures.

Forward, 4th July, 1914

The Volunteers of Grattan's time were betrayed by their leaders, as the Volunteers of our time were betrayed by the Parliamentary Party. The Volunteers of Grattan's time broke up without having consolidated their legislative victory, owing to their leaders' faith in the promises of English statesmen just as the Volunteers of our time were disorganised by the fact of their leaders trust in the promises of English statesmen.

Despite their enthusiasm for Ireland the greatest section of Grattan's Volunteers became active members of the yeomanry who afterwards achieved notoriety for their crimes against Ireland, just as a considerable section of the Volunteers of our day have become soldiers of the English army-active agents of the military army of the oppressors of their country.

Workers' Republic, 8th January, 1916

The revolutionary nationalist worships the ideals and adheres to the methods of the past; Home Rulers profess to worship at the same shrine, but adopt neither the ideals or methods of past revolutionists; and the Socialist Republicans adhere to the high ideal of national freedom sought for in the past, go beyond it to a fuller ideal which we conceive to flow from national freedom as a natural necessary consequence, but reject as utterly unsuited to present conditions the methods of bygone generations.

We agitate for the Revolution; let those who will conspire for it; when the hour for action arrives our only rivalry need be as to which shall strike the most effective blows against the common enemy.

Workers' Republic, 23rd June, 1900

North-East Ulster

I have explained before how the perfectly devilish ingenuity of the master class had sought its ends in North-East Ulster; how the land was stolen from Catholics, given to Episcopalians, but planted by Presbyterians; how the latter were persecuted by the Government, but could not avoid the necessity of defending it against the Catholics, and how out of this complicated situation there inevitably grew up a feeling of common interests between the slaves and the slave-drivers.

As the march of the Irish towards emancipation developed, as step by step they secured more and more political rights and greater and greater recognition, so in like ratio the disabilities of the Presbyterians and other dissenters were abolished.

For a brief period during the closing years of the eighteenth century, it did indeed seem probable that the common disabilities of Presbyterians and Catholics would unite them all under the common name of Irishmen. Hence the rebel society of that time took the significant name of "United Irishmen". But the removal of the religious disabilities from the dissenting community had, as its effect, the obliteration of all political difference between the sects and their practical political unity under the common designation of Protestants, as against the Catholics, upon whom the fetters of religious disability still clung.

Forward, 2nd August, 1913

Humanly speaking, one would have confidently predicted that as the Presbyterians and Dissenters were emancipated as a result of a clamorous agitation against religious inequality, and as that agitation derived its chief force and menace from the power of Catholic numbers in Ireland, then the members of these sects would unite with the agitators to win for all an enjoyment of these rights the agitators and rebels had won for them.

But the prediction would have missed the mark by several million miles. Instead, the Protestants who had been persecuted joined with the Protestants who had persecuted them against the menace of an intrusion by the Catholics into the fold of political and religious freedom - "Civil and religious liberty".

There is no use blaming them. It is common experience in history that as each order fought its way upward into the circle of governing classes, it joined with its former tyrants in an endeavour to curb the aspirations of these orders still unfree.

That in Ireland religious sects played the same game as elsewhere was played by economic or social classes does not prove the wickedness of the Irish players, but does serve to illustrate the universality of the passions that operate upon the stage of the world's history.

Ibid.

If the North-East corner of Ireland is, therefore, the home of a people whose minds are saturated with conceptions of political activity fit only for the atmosphere of the seventeenth century, if the sublime ideas of an all-embracing democracy equally as insistent upon its duties as upon its rights have as yet found poor lodgement here, the fault lies not with this generation of toilers, but with those pastors and masters who deceived it and enslaved it in the past - and deceived it in order that they might enslave it.

But as no good can come of blaming it, so also no good, but infinite evil, can come of truckling to it. Let the truth be told, however ugly. Here, the Orange working class are slaves in spirits because they have been reared up among a people whose conditions of servitude were more slavish than their own. In Catholic Ireland the working class are rebels in spirit and democratic in feeling because for hundreds of years they have found no class as lowly paid or as hardly treated as themselves.

Ibid.

Here in Ireland the proposal of the Government to consent to the partition of Ireland - the exclusion of certain counties in Ulster - is causing a new line of cleavage. No one of the supporters of Home Rule accepts this proposal with anything like equanimity, but rather we are already hearing in North-East Ulster rumours of a determination to resist it by all means. It is felt that the proposal to leave the Home Rule minority at the mercy of an ignorant majority with the evil record of the Orange party is a proposal that should never have been made, and that the establishment of such a scheme should be resisted with armed force if necessary.

Personally I entirely agree with those who think so; Belfast is bad enough as it is; what it would be under such rule the wildest imagination cannot conceive. Filled with the belief that they were after defeating the Imperial Government and the Nationalists combined, the Orangemen would have scant regard for the rights of the minority left at their mercy.

Such a scheme would destroy the Labour movement by disrupting it. It would perpetuate in a form aggravated in evil the discords now prevalent, and help the Home Rule and Orange capitalists and clerics to keep their rallying cries before the public as the political watchwords of the day. In short, it would make division more intense and confusion of ideas and parties more confounded.

Forward, 21st March, 1914

Now, what is the position of Labour towards it all? Let us remember that the Orange aristocracy now fighting for its supremacy in Ireland has at all times been based upon a denial of the common human rights of the Irish people; that the Orange Order was not founded to safeguard religious freedom, but to deny religious freedom, and that it raised this religious question, not for the sake of any religion, but in order to use religious zeal in the interests of the oppressive property rights of rack-renting landlords and sweating capitalists. That the Irish people might be kept asunder and robbed whilst so sundered and divided, the Orange aristocracy went down to the lowest depths and out of the lowest pits of Hell brought up the abominations of sectarian feuds to stir the passions of the ignorant mob. No crime was too brutal or cowardly; no lie too base; no slander too ghastly, as long as they served to keep the democracy asunder.

Irish Worker, 14th March, 1914

Such a scheme as that agreed to by Redmond and Devlin, the betrayal of the national democracy of industrial Ulster would mean a carnival of reaction both North and South, would set back the wheels of progress, would destroy the oncoming unity of the Irish Labour movement and paralyse all advanced movements whilst it endured.

To it Labour should give the bitterest opposition, against it Labour in Ulster should fight even to the death, if necessary, as our fathers fought before us.

Ibid.

The reader will also see that with a perfectly Mephistophelian subtlety the question of exclusion is not suggested to be voted upon by any large area where the chances for or against might be fairly equal, where exclusion might be defeated as it might be if all Ulster were the venue of the poll, and all Ulster had to stay out or come in as a result of the verdict of the ballot box. No, the counties to be voted on the question are the counties where the Unionists are in an overwhelming majority, and where therefore the vote is a mere farce - a subterfuge to hide the grossness of the betrayal of the Home Rule electors.

Forward, 11th April, 1914

In this great crisis of the history of Ireland, I desire to appeal to the working class - the only class whose true interests are always on the side of progress - to take action to prevent the betrayal of their interests contemplated by those who have planned the exclusion of part of Ulster from the Home Rule Bill. Every effort is now being made to prevent the voice of the democracy being heard in those counties and boroughs which it is callously proposed to cut off from the rest of Ireland. Meetings are being rushed through in other parts of Ireland, and at those meetings wirepullers of the United Irish League and the Ancient Order of Hibernians (Board of Erin) are passing resolutions approving of the exclusion, whilst you who will suffer by this dastardly proposal are never even consulted, but, on the contrary, these same organisations are working hard to prevent your voice being heard, and have done what they could to prevent the calling of meetings, of holding of demonstrations at which you could register your hatred of their attempt to betray you into the hand of the sworn enemies of democracy, of labour, and of nationality.

Irish Worker, 4th April, 1914

Do not be misled by the promises of politicians. Remember that Mr. Birrell, Chief Secretary, solemnly promised that a representative of Dublin Labour would sit upon the Police Inquiry Commission in Dublin, and that he broke his solemn promise. Remember that Mr. Redmond pledged his word at Waterford that the Home Rule Bill would go through without the loss of a word or a comma, and almost immediately afterwards he agreed to the loss of four counties and two boroughs. Remember that the whole history of Ireland is a record of betrayals by politicians and statesmen, and remembering this, spurn their lying promises and stand up for a United Ireland - an Ireland broad based upon the union of Labour and Nationality.

Ibid.

You are not frightened by the mock heroics of a pantomime army. Nobody in Ulster is. If the politicians in Parliament pretend to be frightened, it is only in order to find an excuse to sell you. Do not be sold. Remember that when soldiers were ordered out to shoot you down in the Belfast Dock Strike of 1907, no officer resigned then rather than shed blood in Ulster, and when some innocent members of our class were shot down in the Falls Road, Belfast, no Cabinet Ministers apologised to the relatives of the poor workers they had murdered. Remember that more than a thousand Dublin men, women and children were brutally beaten and wounded by the police a few months ago, and three men and one girl killed, but no officer resigned, and neither Tory nor Home Rule press protested against the coercion of Dublin. Why, then, the hypocritical howl against compelling the pious sweaters of Ulster and their dupes to obey the will of the majority? Remember the A.O.H., the U.I.L. and the Irish Parliamentary Party cheered on the Government when it sent its police to bludgeon the Nationalist workers of Dublin.

Ibid.

As the officers of the Curragh have stood by their class, so let the working-class democracy of Ulster stand by its class, and all Irish workers from Malin Head to Cape Clear and from Dublin to Galway will stand by you.

Let your motto be that of James Fintan Lalor, the motto which the working class Irish Citizen Army has adopted as its aim and object, *viz:* That the entire ownership of Ireland (All Ireland) - moral and material – is vested of right in the entire people of Ireland.

And, adopting this as your motto, let it be heard and understood that Labour in Ireland stands for the unity of Ireland - an Ireland united in the name of progress, and who shall separate us?

Ibid.

Charles Stewart Parnell could have got Home Rule with Ulster excluded thirty years ago. We have been told ad nauseum about the statesmanlike qualities of John E. Redmond as the leader of the Irish race, and yet it appears that his statesmanship has brought his followers to the point of accepting with joyful eagerness and gratitude that which Parnell rejected with scorn thirty years ago. A more miserable fiasco than this ignominious collapse of a great national movement is not recorded in history.

Forward, 18th April, 1914

A Cabinet Minister, Mr. Winston Churchill, announces that he has accepted an invitation from Ulster Liberals to address a Home Rule meeting in the Ulster Hall in Belfast. A meeting of the Ulster Unionist Council, with a noble lord in the chair, publicly announces that it will take steps to prevent Mr. Churchill's meeting. Up to that point nobody in Ulster who knows the Ulstermen had taken in the least degree seriously the threats of fighting on their part. All recognised that the rank and file were probably ready enough to fight, but all also recognised that the economic position of the leaders of the Orange forces, their standing as holders of capitalist stock, land, coal mines, shipping, etc., made the suggestion that they should rebel against the Government that guaranteed their investments - a very ridiculous suggestion indeed. It was generally felt that a firm application of the power of the police force would suffice to quell in a few days all the Orange resistance, and nobody dreamt that the Government would hesitate in firmly applying that force upon the first opportunity. Any open defiance of the law, any open declaration of an intention to break the laws, supplied just that opportunity for the Government to act with all the traditions of law and order at its back... All the traditions of British constitutional procedure were outraged; even the most hardened Tories in Great Britain looked askance at this Orange proposal to deny to a Cabinet Minister that right of public meeting theoretically allowed to even the most irresponsible agitator. The occasion called, and called loudly, for a firm application of force to establish, once and for all, the right of public meeting in Ulster; to convince the Orange hosts that henceforth unpopular opinion must be met by arguments and not by bolts, rivets, nuts or weapons of war.

But, lo and behold! the Government ran away. Mr. Winston Churchill abandoned his right to hold his meeting in the place advertised, and slunk away to the outskirts of the city to hold a meeting surrounded by more soldiers and police than would have sufficed to capture the city if held by the whole Orange forces in battle array. We in Ulster gasped with astonishment at this pitiful surrender of public liberties, and we realised that a direct encouragement had been given to all the forces of reaction to pursue the path of violence.

Forward, 30th May, 1914

Next in importance to the abandonment of the right of public meeting came the tacit permission given to the Ulster Volunteers to arm themselves with the avowed object of resisting the law.

For two years this arming went on, accompanied by drilling and organising upon a military basis, and no effort was made to stop the drilling or to prevent the free importation of arms until the example of the Ulster Volunteers began to be followed through the rest of Ireland.

Ibid.

My firm conviction is that the Liberal Government wish to betray the Home Rulers, that they connive at these illegalities that they might have an excuse for their betrayal, and that the Home Rule party through its timidity and partly through its hatred of Labour in Ireland is incapable of putting the least pressure upon its Liberal allies and must now dance to the piping of its treacherous allies.

Ibid.

According to all Socialist theories North-East Ulster, being the most developed industrially, ought to be the quarter in which class lines of cleavage, politically and industrially, should be the most pronounced and class rebellion the most common.

As a cold matter of fact, it is the happy hunting ground of the slave-driver and the home of the least rebellious slaves in the Industrial world.

Dublin, on the other hand, has more strongly developed working-class feeling, more strongly accentuated instincts of loyalty to the working class than any city of its size in the globe.

Forward, 2nd August, 1913

Of late, sections of the advanced Nationalist press have lent themselves to a desperate effort to misrepresent the position of the Carsonites, and to claim for them the admiration of Irish Nationalists on the grounds that these Carsonites were fearless Irishmen who had refused to take dictation from England. A more devilishly mischievous and lying doctrine was never preached in Ireland. The Carsonite position is indeed plain - so plain that nothing but sheer perversity of purpose can misunderstand it, or cloak it with a resemblance to Irish patriotism. The Carsonites say that their fathers were planted in this country to assist in keeping the natives down in subjection that this country might be held for England. That this was God's will because the Catholic Irish were not fit for the responsibilities and powers of free men and that they are not fit for the exercise of these responsibilities and powers till this day. Therefore, say the Carsonites, we have kept our side of the bargain; we have refused to admit the Catholics to power and responsibility; we have manned the government of this country for England, we propose to continue to do so, and rather than admit that these Catholics - these "mickies and teagues" - are our equals, we will fight, in the hope that our fighting will cause the English people to revolt against their government and re-establish us in our historic position as an English colony in Ireland, superior to, and unhampered by, the political institutions of the Irish natives.

How this can be represented as the case of Irishmen refusing to take dictation from England passeth all comprehension.

Irish Worker, 8th August, 1914

Socialism, Religion and Clergymen

I have long been of the opinion that the socialist movement elsewhere was to a great extent hampered by the presence in its ranks of faddists and cranks, who were in the movement, not for the cause of socialism, but because they thought they saw in it a means of ventilating their theories on such questions as sex, religion, vaccination, vegetarianism, etc., and I believed that such ideas had or ought to have no place in our programme or in our party...

The Socialist, June, 1904

Socialism is an industrial and political question; it is going to be settled in the workshops and at the ballot boxes of this and every other country and is not going to be settled at the altar. The education which fits a man for the altar does not give him mastery over economic knowledge. The priest who has even studied for his priesthood at Rome usually could learn a lot about modern industry from the Irish labourer whose childhood, manhood and old age are spent toiling in workshop, mine or factory for a starvation wage.

The Harp, June, 1908

There are quite a few people who believe that his Eminence (Cardinal Logue of Armagh) stands for conceptions of human society, and holds ideas on intellectual development that properly belong to the darkest of dark ages, and make him a greater menace to free American institutions than the most violent Anarchist that ever was barred out of the United States... The time has long since gone by when Irish men and Irish women could be kept from thinking by hurling priestly thunder at their heads. We may still kneel to the Servant of God, but when he speaks as the Servant of our Oppressors he must not wonder if he receives from slaves in revolt the same measure as his earthly masters. It is well to let His Eminence, Cardinal Logue, know that he cannot act the despot and throttle the press in Ireland, and act the patron of free institutions in America without the slight difference of attitude causing some comment. It is well, above all, to let all the clerical ranters (Protestant and Catholic) against Socialism realise that it is not Socialism that is on trial before the bar of advancing civilisation, but they and theirs...

The Harp, May, 1908

Our minds travel back to the early days of the Irish Land League, the attitude of the clergy of Ireland towards that uprising of the poor, and the great change in their attitude when that movement became a dominent force in the struggle between landlord and tenant. In the early days the higher clergy had practically nothing but condemnation for the agitation and vehement denunciation of the agitators, and needless to say the denunciations indulged in by bishops were so often zealously improved upon by the lurid oratory of parish priests and curates who wished to become parish priests...

Irish Worker, 6th July, 1912

For the present, it is sufficient to emphasise the fact that the religious affiliations of the population of Ulster determine their political leanings to a greater extent than is the case in any part of Europe outside the Balkans.

But the manner in which this has developed is also unique. I believe that it is true to say that, politically speaking, the Protestantism of the North of Ireland has no parallel outside this country, and that the Catholicism of the Irish Catholics is, likewise, peculiar in its political trend.

To explain - I mean that, whereas, Protestantism has in general made for political freedom and political Radicalism, it has been opposed to slavish worship of kings and aristocrats. Here, in Ireland, the word Protestant is almost a convertible term with Toryism, lickspittle loyalty, servile worship of aristocracy and hatred of all that savours of genuine political independence on the part of the "lower classes". And in the same manner, Catholicism which in most parts of Europe is synonymous with Toryism, lickspittle loyalty, servile worship of aristocracy and hatred of all that savours of genuine political independence on the part of the lower classes, in Ireland is almost synonymous with rebellious tendencies, zeal for democracy, and intense feeling of solidarity with all strivings upward of those who toil.

Forward, 3rd May, 1913

Let me also add that it is about time in their own interests that the clergy began to study what socialism really is. I have read a good many scare fulminations against socialism from his Holiness down and I have never seen but one from such a source that showed any real knowledge of what socialism really is.

The Harp, October, 1908

As a matter of fact the Catholic Church always accepts the established order, even if it has warred upon those who had striven to establish such order.

To use a homely adage the Church "does not put all her eggs in one basket", and the man who imagines that in the supreme hour of the proletarian struggle for victory the Church will definitely line up with the forces of capitalism, and pledge her very existence as a Church upon the hazardous chance of the capitalists winning, simply does not understand the first thing about the policy of the Church in the social or political revolutions of the past. Just as in Ireland the Church denounced every Irish revolutionary movement in its day of activity, as in 1798, 1848 and 1867, and yet allowed its priests to deliver speeches in eulogy of the active spirits of those movements a generation afterwards, so in the future the Church, which has its hand close upon the pulse of human society, when it realises that the cause of capitalism is a lost cause it will find excuse enough to allow freedom of speech and expression to those lowly priests whose socialist declarations it will then use to cover and hide the absolute anti-socialism of the Roman Propaganda. When that day comes the Papal Encyclical against socialism will be conveniently forgotten by the Papal historians, and the socialist utterances of the von Kettelers, the McGlynns, and McGradys will be heralded forth and the communistic utterances of the early fathers as proofs of Catholic sympathy with progressive ideas.

The Harp, September, 1908

Socialism, as a party, bases itself upon its knowledge of facts, of economic truths, and leaves the building up of religious ideals or faiths to the outside public, or to its individual members if they so will. It is neither Freethinker nor Christian, Turk nor Jew, Buddhist nor Idolater, Mahommedan nor Parsee - it is only human.

Workers' Republic, 17th June, 1899

It seems to be unavoidable, but it is entirely regrettable, that clergymen consecrated to the worship of God, and supposed to be patterned after a Redeemer who was the embodiment of service and humility, should in their relations to the laity insist upon service and humility being rendered to them instead of by them. Their Master served all mankind in patience and suffering; they insist upon all mankind serving them, and in all questions of the social and political relationships of men they require the common laity to bow the neck in a meekness, humility, and submission which the clergy scornfully reject. They have often insisted that the Church is greater than the secular authority, and acted therefore in flat defiance of the secular powers, but they have forgotten or ignored the fact that the laity are a part of the Church, and that therefore the right of rebellion against injustice so freely claimed by the Papacy and the hierarchy is also the inalienable right of the laity. And history proves that in almost every case in which the political or social aspirations of the laity came into opposition to the will of the clergy the laity represented the best interest of the Church as a whole and of mankind in general. Whenever the clergy succeeded in conquering political power in any country the result has been disastrous to the interests of religion and inimical to the progress of humanity. From whence we arrive at the conclusion that he serves religion best who insists upon the clergy of the Catholic Church taking their proper position as servants to the laity, and abandoning their attempt to dominate the public, as they have long dominated the private life of their fellow-Catholics.

Labour, Nationality & Religion, 1910

Most of our readers are aware that the first Anglo-Norman invasion of Ireland, in 1169, an invasion characterised by every kind of treachery, outrage, and indiscriminate massacre of the Irish, took place under the authority of a bull issued by his Holiness, Pope Adrian IV. Doubt has been cast upon the authenticity of the bull, but it is certain that neither Adrian nor any of his successors in the Papal chair ever repudiated it.

Ibid.

Every Irish man and woman, most enlightened Englishmen, and practically every foreign nation today wish that the Irish had succeeded in preserving their independence against the English King, Henry II, but at a Synod of the Catholic Church, held in Dublin in 1177, according to Rev. P.J. Carew, Professor of Divinity in Maynooth, in his *Ecclesiastical History of Ireland*, the Legate of Pope Alexander III "set forth Henry's right to the sovereignty of Ireland in virtue of the Pope's authority, and inculcated the necessity of obeying him under pain of excommunication". The English were not yet eight years in Ireland, the greater part of the country was still closed to them, but already the Irish were being excommunicated for refusing to become slaves.

Ibid.

The Battle of the Boyne, fought 1st July, 1690, is generally regarded in Ireland as a disaster for the Irish cause - a disaster which made possible the infliction of two centuries of unspeakable degradation upon the Irish people. Yet that battle was the result of an alliance formed by Pope Innocent XI with William, Prince of Orange, against Louis, King of France. King James of England joined with King Louis to obtain help to save his own throne, and the Pope joined in the league with William to curb the power of France. When the news of the defeat of the Irish at the Boyne reached Rome the Vatican was illuminated by order of the new Pope, Alexander VIII, and special Masses offered up in thanksgiving.

Ibid.

In 1798 an insurrection in favour of an Irish Republic took place in Ireland, assuming most formidable proportions in County Wexford. The insurrection had been planned by the Society of United Irishmen, many of whose leaders were Protestants and Freethinkers. The Catholic Hierarchy and most of the priesthood denounced the society and inculcated loyalty to the Government. The more intelligent of the Catholic masses disregarded these clerical denunciations. In the memoirs of his life, Miles Byrne, a staunch Catholic patriot and revolutionist, who took part in the insurrection, says, "The priests did everything in their power to stop the progress of the Association of United Irishmen, particularly poor Father John Redmond, who refused to hear the confession of any of the United Irish, and turned them away from his knees." Speaking of Father John Murphy, he says he " was a worthy, simple, pious man, and one of those Roman Catholic priests who used the greatest exertions and exhortations to oblige the people to give up their pikes and firearms of every description." The wisdom of the people and the foolishness of the clergy were amply demonstrated by the fact that the soldiers burned Father Murphy's house over his head, and compelled him to take the field as an insurgent. A heroic fight and a glorious martyrdom atoned for his mistake, but the soldier-like qualities he showed in the field were rendered nugatory by the fact that as a priest he had been instrumental in disarming many hundreds of the men whom he afterwards commanded. As an insurgent officer he discovered that his greatest hope lay in the men who had disregarded his commands as a priest, and retained the arms with which to fight for freedom.

Ibid.

The Irish revolutionary movement known popularly as the Fenian Brotherhood was denounced by all the Catholic Hierarchy and most of the clergy, Bishop Moriarty of County Kerry saying that "Hell was not hot enough nor eternity long enough to punish such miscreants." The Fenians were represented as being enemies of religion and of morality, yet the three representatives of their cause who died upon the scaffold died with a prayer upon their lips, and Irish men and women the world over today make the anniversary of their martyrdom the occasion for a glorification and endorsement of the principles for which they died - a glorification and endorsement in which many of our clergymen participate.

Ibid.

On 11th May, 1883, in the midst of the the fight of the Irish peasantry to save themselves from landlord tyranny, his Holiness the Pope issued a Rescript condemning disaffection to the English Government and also condemning the testimonial to Charles Stewart Parnell. The Irish people answered by more than doubling the subscription to the testimonial. The leader of that fight of the Irish against their ancient tyrants was Michael Davitt, to whose efforts much of the comparative security of peasant life in Ireland is due. Davitt was denied an audience by the Pope but at his death priests and people alike united to do tribute to his character and genius.

Ibid.

The divorce evil of today arises not out of Socialist teaching, but out of that capitalist system whose morals and philosophy are based upon the idea of individualism, and the cash nexus as the sole bond in society. Such teaching destroys the sanctity of the marriage bond, and makes of love and the marriage bed things to be bought and sold. Can it be wondered at that such teaching as that which exalts the individual pursuit of riches as the absolutely necessary cement of society should produce a loosening of all social bonds, including that of marriage, and threaten to suffocate society with the stench of its own rottenness? Yet it is such capitalist ethics and practice our priests and prelates are defending, and it is of such that Father Kane arises as the champion and expounder.

Ibid.

Yet this is what Father Kane said:

"Divorce in the Socialist sense means that woman would be willing to stoop to be the mistress of one man after another." A more unscrupulous slander upon womanhood was never uttered or penned. Remember that this was said in Ireland, and do you not wonder that some Irish women - some persons of the same sex as the slanderer's mother - did not get up and hurl the lie back in his teeth, and tell him that it was not law which kept them virtuous, that if all marriage laws were abolished to-morrow, it would not make women "willing to stoop to be the mistress of one man after another." Aye, verily, the uncleanness lies not in this alleged Socialist proposal, but in the minds of those who so interpret it. The inability of Father Kane to appreciate the innate morality of womanhood, and the superiority of the morals of the women of the real people to that of the class he is defending, recalls to mind the fact that the Council of the Church held at Mâcon in the sixth century gravely debated the question as to whether women had or had not a soul, and that the affirmation that she had was only carried by a small majority. Many of the early Fathers of the Church were, indeed, so bitter in their denunciation of women and of marriage that their opinions read like the expressions of mad men when examined in the cold light of the twentieth century. Origen said: "Marriage is unholy and unclean - a means of sensual lust." St. Jerome declared: "Marriage is at the least a vice; all that we can do is to excuse and justify it"; and Tertullian, in his hatred of women, thundered forth boldly that which Father Kane dared only insinuate: "Woman," he preaches, "thou oughtest always to walk in mourning and rags, thine eyes filled with tears of repentance to make men forget that Thou hast been the destruction of the race. Woman! Thou art the Gates of Hell." Thus throughout the centuries persists the idea of the churchmen that women can only be kept virtuous by law.

Ibid.

The Socialist doctrine teaches that all men are brothers, that the same red blood of a common humanity flows in the veins of all races, creeds, colours and nations, that the interests of labour are everywhere identical, and that wars are an abomination. Is not this also good Catholic doctrine - the doctrine of a Church which prides itself upon being universal or Catholic? How, then, can that doctrine which is high and holy in theory on the lips of a Catholic become a hissing and a blasphemy when practised by the Socialist? The Socialist does not cease to love his country when he tries to make that country the common property of its people; he rather shows a greater love of country than is shown by those who wish to perpetuate a system which makes the great majority of the people of a country exiles and outcasts, living by sufferance of capitalists and landlords in their native land. Under Socialism we can all voice the saying of the poet; at present "our" native land is in pawn to landlords and capitalists.

Ibid.

Recently there died in Europe a king - King Leopold of Belgium - whose private life was so disgracefully immoral that it was the scandal of Europe. A married man with a grown-up family, he kept a Parisian actress as his mistress, and led so scandalous a life that the females of his family refused to follow his body to the grave. Yet when he died the whole official Catholic world went into mourning for him. He was more of a representative of the institution of monarchy than any private individual can ever be of Socialism; but the Rev. Father Kane or his Holiness the Pope did not therefore deliver sermons against the wickedness of supporting kings. And what is true in these two striking examples is also true of kings, nobles, and capitalists all the world over.

Ibid.

That some Socialists believe that force may be used to inaugurate the new social order only indicates their conviction that the criminal capitalist and ruling classes will not peacefully abide by the verdict of the ballot, but will strive by violence to perpetuate their robber rule in spite of the declared will of the majority of the people. In this conviction such Socialists are strengthened by the record of all the revolutions of the world's history. It is a well established fact that from the earliest revolutionary outbreak known down to the Commune of Paris, or Red Sunday in Russia, the first blood has been shed, the first blow struck, by the possessing conservative classes. And we are not so childish as to imagine that the capitalist class of the future will shrink from the shedding of the blood of the workers in order to retain their ill-gotten gains. They shed more blood, destroy more working class lives every year, by the criminal carelessness with which they conduct industry and drive us to nerve-racking speed, than is lost in the average international war. In the United States there are killed on the railroads in one year more men than died in the Boer War on both sides. When the capitalists kill us so rapidly for the sake of a few pence extra profit it would be suicidal to expect that they would hesitate to slaughter us wholesale when their very existence as parasites was at stake. Therefore, the

Socialists anticipate violence only because they know the evil nature of the beast they contend with.

Ibid.

The day has passed for patching up the capitalist system; it must go. And in the work of abolishing it the Catholic and the Protestant, the Catholic and the Jew, the Catholic and the Freethinker, the Catholic and the Buddhist, the Catholic and the Mohammedan will co-operate together, knowing no rivalry but the rivalry of endeavour toward an end beneficial to all. For, as we have said elsewhere, Socialism is neither Protestant nor Catholic, Christian nor Freethinker, Buddhist, Mohammedan, nor Jew; it is only HUMAN. We of the Socialist working class realise that as we suffer together we must work together that we may enjoy together. We reject the firebrand of capitalist warfare and offer you the olive leaf of brotherhood and justice to and for all.

Ibid.

The Great War

Do not let anyone play upon your sympathies by denunciation of the German military bullies. German military bullies, like all tyrannies among civilised people need fear nothing so much as native (German) democracy. Attacks from outside only strengthen tyrants within a nation.

Irish Worker, 22nd August, 1914

It was determined that since Germany could not be beaten in fair competition industrially, it must be beaten unfairly by organising a military and naval conspiracy against her. British methods and British capitalism might be inferior to German methods and German capitalism; German scientists aided by German workers might be superior to British workers and tardy British science, but the British fleet was still superior to the German in point of numbers and weight of artillery. Hence it was felt that if the German nation could be ringed round with armed foes upon its every frontier until the British fleet could strike at its ocean-going commerce, then German competition would be crushed and the supremacy of England in commerce ensured for another generation. The conception meant calling up the forces of barbaric powers to crush and hinder the development of the peaceful powers of industry. It was a conception worthy of fiends, but what do you expect? You surely do not expect the roses of honour and civilisation to grow on the thorn tree of capitalist competition - and that tree planted in the soil of a British ruling class.

Irish Worker, 29th August, 1914

Yes, friends, governments in capitalist society are but committees of the rich to manage the affairs of the capitalist class. The British capitalist class have planned this colossal crime in order to ensure its uninterrupted domination of the commerce of the world. To achieve that end it is prepared to bathe a continent in blood, to kill off the flower of the manhood of the three most civilised great nations of Europe, to place the iron heel of the Russian tyrant upon the throat of all liberty-loving races and peoples from the Baltic to the Black Sea, and to invite the blessing of God upon the spectacle of the savage Cossack ravishing the daughters of a race at the head of Christian civilisation.

Yes, this war is the war of a pirate upon the German nation.

And up from the blood-soaked graves of the Belgian frontiers the spirits of murdered Irish soldiers of England call to Heaven for vengeance upon the Parliamentarian tricksters who seduced them into the armies of the oppressor of their country.

Ibid.

In these days of conflict Ireland occupies a unique position. For the first time in history an Irish leader has publicly pledged the support of the Irish nation to Great Britain in an armed struggle.

Forward, 5th September, 1914

At first the country seemed quite swept off its feet by this action. All the kept newspapers of the United Irish League immediately constituted themselves recruiting agents for the British Army, and every effort was made to stampede the Volunteers into unconditional acceptance of Mr. Redmond's blatant offer. Many thousands of recruits were obtained for the British Army during the first week or fortnight of the jingo fever promoted by the Home Rule press and wirepullers, companies of Irish Volunteers marched in parade order to see reservists off by the train and ship, their bands, to the astonishment of everyone and the horror of most, played "God Save the King", and all sorts of erstwhile rack-renting landlords and anti-Irish aristocrats rushed in to officer these Irish Volunteers whom they had formerly despised. But gradually the nation is swinging back to sanity. The independent elements are everywhere asserting themselves, and there has already developed a fierce fight to prevent the Irish volunteers being - as Mr. Redmond intended - handed over to the War Office.

Ibid.

Along with this a strong propaganda is being carried on showing that Ireland has no quarrel with the German nation; that on the contrary, Irish culture and Irish literature owe very much indeed to German friendship and to German research.

Ibid.

The Russian Socialists have issued a strong manifesto denouncing the war, and pouring contempt upon the professions of the Czar in favour of oppressed races, pointing out his suppression of the liberties of Finland, his continued martyrdom of Poland, his atrocious tortures and massacres in the Baltic provinces, and his withdrawal of the recently granted parliamentary liberties of Russia. And to that again add the fact that the Polish Nationalists have warned the Poles against putting any faith in a man who has proven himself incapable of keeping his solemnly pledged faith with his own people, and you will begin to get a saner view of the great game that is being played than you can ever acquire from the lying press of Ireland and England.

Irish Worker, 12th September, 1914

Of course, that should not blind you to the splendid stand which the British Government, we are assured, is making against German outrages and brutality and in favour of small nationalities. The Russian Government is admitted by every publicist in England to be a foul blot upon civilisation. It was but the other day that when the Russian Duma was supressed by force and many of its elected representatives imprisoned and exiled, an English Cabinet Minister defiantly declared in public, in spite of international courtesies:

"The Duma is dead! Long live the Duma!"

But all that is forgotten now, and the Russian Government and the British Government stand solidly together in favour of small nationalities everywhere except in countries now under Russian and British rule.

Ibid.

Yes, I seem to remember a small country called Egypt, a country that through ages of servitude has painfully evolved to a conception of national freedom, and under leaders of its own choosing essayed to make that conception a reality. And I think I remember how this British friend of small nationalities bombarded its chief seaport, invaded and laid waste its territory, slaughtered its armies, imprisoned its citizens, led its chosen leaders away in chains, and reduced the new-born Egyptian nation into a conquered, servile British province.

Ibid.

When I read the attempts of the prize Irish press to work up feeling against the Germans by talk of German outrages at the front, I wonder if those who swallow such yarns ever remember the facts about the exploits of the British generals in South Africa. When we are told of the horrors of Louvain, when the only damage that was done was the result of civilians firing upon German troops from buildings which those troops had in consequence to attack, I remember that in South Africa Lord Roberts issued an order that whenever there was an attack upon the railways in his line of communication every Boer house and farmstead within a radius of ten square miles had to be destroyed.

Ibid.

When I hear of the unavoidable killing of civilians in a line of battle 100 miles long in a densely populated country, being of, as it were, part of the German plan of campaign, I remember how the British swept up the whole non-combatant Boer population into concentration camps, and kept it there until the little children died in thousands of fever and cholera; so that the final argument in causing the Boers to make peace was the fear that at the rate of infant mortality in those concentration camps there would be no new generation left to inherit the republic for which their elders were fighting.

Ibid.

War is ever the enemy of progress. It is only possible when humanity is stifled, when the common interests of the human race are denied. The first blast of the bugles of war is also the requiem note of human brotherhood. It is but a step, and a short step, from exulting in the sufferings of a foreign enemy to contemptuous indifference to the sights and sounds of suffering amongst our own poor in our own streets. The poor of the world would be well advised, upon the declaration of war in any country, as their first steps to peace, to hang the Foreign Minister and Cabinet whose secret diplomacy produced such a result. If each country hanged its own Foreign Minister and Cabinet before setting out to the front, wars would not last long; and if a jingo editor were hanged each week it lasted, the most jingo being the first to hang, not many angry passions would be stirred up to make the work of peaceful understanding difficult.

Irish Worker, 14th November, 1914

We know that not more than a score of men in the various Cabinets of the world have brought about this war, that no European people was consulted upon the question, that preparations for it have been going on for years, and that all the alleged "reasons" for it are so many afterthoughts invented to hide from us the fact that the intrigues and schemes of our rulers had brought the world to this pass. All socialists are agreed upon this. Being so agreed, are we now to forget it all: to forget all our ideas of human brotherhood, and because some twenty highly-placed criminals say our country requires us to slaughter our brothers beyond the seas or the frontiers, are we bound to accept their statement, and proceed to slaughter our comrades abroad at the dictate of our enemies at home.

Forward, 22nd August, 1914

The war of a subject nation for independence, for the right to live out its own life in its own way may and can be justified as holy and righteous; the war of a subject class to free itself from the debasing conditions of economic and political slavery should at all times choose its own weapons, and hold and esteem all as sacred instruments of righteousness. But the war of nation against nation in the interest of royal freebooters and cosmopolitan thieves is a thing accursed.

Ibid.

We have held, and do hold, that war is a relic of barbarism only possible because we are governed by a ruling class with barbaric ideas; we have held and do hold that the working class of all countries cannot hope to escape the horrors of war until in all countries that barbaric ruling class is thrown from power; and we have held, and do hold that the lust for power on the part of that ruling class is so deeply rooted in the nature and instinct of its members, that it is more than probable that nothing less than superior force will ever induce them to abandon their throttling grasp upon the lives and liberties of mankind.

The Worker, 30th January, 1915

I believe the war could have been prevented by the socialists; as it was not prevented and as the issues are knit, I want to see England beaten so thoroughly that the commerce of the seas will henceforth be free to all nations - to the smallest equally with the greatest.

International Socialist Review, March, 1915

The sons of Ireland who are in arms are in arms for England, the blood of Ireland that flows in torrents every day flows for England, the Irish men who die fighting like heroes and demigods die fighting for England. Ireland knows them not, can never number them amongst her possessions, can never tell the tale of their sufferings and exploits as sufferings and exploits for her.

Workers' Republic, 31st July, 1915

And yet Ireland dare not blame them! The least of these, our brothers, would have fought for Ireland if those who spoke in Ireland's name had but had the courage to call them, to summon them to the sacrifice. But all, all failed in the supreme moment of destiny. And it seems to us that when the eternal reckoning is made, God in His infinite wisdom will deal less harshly with the Irish Tommies in the English service than He will with the unscrupulous politicians, or blatant revolutionaries, who stood by in silence and let our poor brothers march out to their fruitless marytrdom in Flanders or the Dardanelles.

Ibid.

Is it not as clear as the fact of life itself that no insurrection of the working class, no general strike, no general uprising of the forces of Labour in Europe, could possibly carry with it, or entail a greater slaughter of socialists, than will their participation as soldiers in the campaigns of the armies of their respective countries?

Every shell which explodes in the midst of a German battalion will slaughter some socialists; every Austrian cavalry charge will leave the gashed and hacked bodies of Serbian or Russian socialists squirming and twisting in agony upon the ground; every Russian, Austrian, or German ship sent to the bottom or blown sky-high will mean sorrow and mourning in the homes of some socialist comrades of ours. If these men must die,would it not be better to die in their own country fighting for freedom for their class, and for the abolition of war, than to go forth to strange countries and die slaughtering and slaughtered by their brothers that tyrants and profiteers might live?

Forward, 15th August, 1914

A great continental uprising of the working class would stop the war; a universal protest at public meetings will not save a single life from being wantonly slaughtered.

Ibid.

I make no war upon patriotism; never have done. But against the patriotism of capitalism - the patriotism which makes the interest of the capitalist class the supreme test of duty and right - I place the patriotism of the working class, the patriotism which judges every public act by its effect upon the fortunes of those who toil. That which is good for the working class I esteem patriotic, but that party or movement is the most perfect embodiment of patriotism which most successfully works for the conquest by the working class of the control of the destinies of the land wherein they labour.

Ibid.

To me, therefore, the socialist of another country is a fellow patriot, as the capitalist of my own country is a natural enemy. I regard each nation as a possessor of a definite contribution to the common stock of civilisation, and I regard the capitalist class of each nation as being the logical and natural enemy of the national culture which constitutes that definite contribution.

Therefore, the stronger I am in my affection for national tradition, literature, language and sympathies, the more firmly rooted I am in my opposition to that capitalist class which in its soulless lust for power and gold would bray the nations as in a mortar.

Reasoning from such premises, therefore, this war appears to me as the most fearful crime of the centuries.

Ibid.

Election Addresses

Having been again asked to contest the Wood Quay Ward in the interests of labour, I desire, in accepting this invitation, to lay before you a few of the principles upon which I conducted the campaign last election, and on which I shall fight this.

Our defeat of last year, brought about as it was by a campaign of slander and bribery, and a wholesale and systematic debauching of the more degraded portion of the electorate, did not in the slightest degree affect the truth of the principles for which we contested. These principles still remain the only principles by which the working class can ever attain its freedom.

Wood Quay Ward, Election Address, January, 1903

When the workers come into the world we find that we are outcasts in the world. The land on which we must live is the property of a class who are the descendants of men who stole the land from our forefathers, and we who are workers, are, whether in town or in country, compelled to pay for permission to live on the earth; the houses, shops, factories, etc., which were built by the labour of our fathers at wages that simply kept them alive are now owned by a class which never contributed an ounce of sweat to their erecting, but whose members will continue to draw rent and profit from them while the system lasts. As a result of this the worker in order to live must sell himself into the service of a master - he must sell to that master the liberty to coin into profit the physical and mental energies.

Ibid.

There is only one remedy for this slavery of the working class, and that remedy is the socialist republic, a system of society in which the land and all houses, railways, factories, canals, workshops, and everything necessary for work shall be owned and operated as common property, much as the land of Ireland was owned by the clans of Ireland before England introduced the capitalist system amongst us at the point of the sword. There is only one way to attain that end, and that way is for the working class to establish a political party of its own; a political party which shall set itself to elect to all public bodies in Ireland working men resolved to use all the power of those bodies for the workers and against their oppressors, whether those oppressors be English, Scotch, or sham Irish patriots.

Ibid.

Let us remember how the paid canvassers of the capitalist candidate - hired slanderers - gave a different account of Mr. Connolly to every section of the electors. How they said to the Catholics that he was an Orangeman, to the Protestants that he was a Fenian, to the Jews that he was an anti-Semite, to others that he was a Jew, to the labourers that he was a journalist on the make, and to the tradesmen and professional classes that he was an ignorant labourer, that he was born in Belfast, Derry, England, Scotland and Italy, according to the person the canvasser was talking to. Remember that all this carnival of corruption and dishonesty was resorted to, simply in order to prevent labour from electing a representative who could neither be bought, terrified nor seduced, and you will understand how important your masters conceive to be their hold on the public bodies in this country. You will also understand that there can never be either clean, healthy, or honest politics in the City of Dublin, until the power of the drink-sellers is absolutely broken - they are positively the meanest and most degraded section that ever attempted to rule a city.

Ibid.

Now, Ladies and Gentlemen, you understand my position. This is socialist republicanism, the politics of labour, of freedom from all tyrants, foreign and native. If you are a worker your interests should compel you to vote for me, if you are a decent citizen, whether worker or master you should vote for me; if you are an enemy of freedom, a tyrant, or the tool of a tyrant, you will vote against me.

Believing that in this fight I am fighting the fight of my class, I invite every self-respecting worker to join our committee and help the cause.

Ibid.

My general attitude, if elected, will be to insist upon the importance of the interests of labour being studied; that wherever possible all Corporation work be done by direct employment of labour; that the trade union clause be enforced in all Corporation contracts; that a minimum wage of at least 6d. per hour be established for all Corporation employees; that membership in a trade union be made compulsory for all wage-earners in Corporation employment; and that the Tramways Committee and its manager be compelled to supply covered cars for workers, morning and evening.

Election Address, Dock Ward, Belfast, January 1913

I stand as a labour candidate, totally independent of any political party. But as the personal views of a candidate cannot be ignored - and as mine are likely to be misrepresented - I judge it well to state mine here that I may at least be heard in my own defence.

Ibid.

Believing that the present system of society is based upon the robbery of the working class, and that capitalist property cannot exist without the plundering of labour, I desire to see capitalism abolished, and a democratic system of common or public ownership erected in its stead. This democratic system, which is called socialism, will, I believe, come as a result of the continuous increase of power of the working class. Only by this means can we secure the abolition of destitution, and all the misery, crime, and immorality which flow from that unnecessary evil. All the reform legislation of the present day is moving in that direction even now, but working class action on above lines will secure that direct, voluntary, conscious, and orderly co-operation by all for the good of all, will more quickly replace the blundering and often reluctant legislation of capitalist governments.

As a lifelong advocate of national independence for Ireland, I am in favour of Home Rule, and believe that Ireland should be ruled, governed, and owned by the people of Ireland.

Ibid.

Fellow workers: I leave my case in your hands. As a trade union official, I stand for the class to which I belong. If you are content to be represented by men belonging to some section of the master class, then do not vote for me, but if you want your cause represented from Dock Ward by one of your own class, who will battle for your rights, who is the determined enemy of the domination of class over class, of nation over nation, of sex over sex, who will at all times stand for the cause of the lowly paid and oppressed, then vote for

Yours fraternally,
James Connolly

Ibid.

Tributes

When we honour Rossa we honour in him the fearless representative of a great movement - a movement that accomplished great things. We honour the latest of those who in days of darkness pledged their faith to an Irish Republic, and kept that faith unsullied to the last.

We on our part affirm that we march behind the remains because we are prepared to fight for the same ideals. And we shall be all the more nerved for fight when we remember that the banner of Fenianism was upheld by the stalwart hands of the Irish working class of that day, as the militant organisation of the same class today is the only body that without reservation unhesitatingly announces its loyalty to the republican principle of national freedom for which the Fenians stood. We are here because this is our place!

Workers' Republic, 31st July, 1915

The (Terence Bellew) MacManus funeral was the first sign of the uprising of Irish Nationality after the shameful, sorrowful days of 1847-48 and 1849. Ireland, in the words of James Fintan Lalor, "sank and surrendered to the famine", and with no resistance of the importance even of a riot had gone down before the blows of the enemy. So completely had she gone down that many of her rebels formally gave up the struggle, and announced their belief that the cause of Ireland's separate existence was a lost cause.

Workers' Republic, 7th August, 1915

Old medieval legends tell us how in the critical moments of the struggle of an army, or the travail of a nation, some angel or deliverer was sent from above to save those favoured by the Most High. To many people today it seems that the funeral of O'Donovan Rossa came to Ireland in such a moment of national agony - came on such a mission of divine uplifting and deliverance. The mists and doubts, the corruption and poisons, the distrust and the treacheries were blown away, and the true men and women of Ireland saw with pleasure the rally of the nation to the olden ideas - saw the real people of the country solemnly bearing witness to the faith and wisdom of those who had "fought a good fight and kept the faith".

The McManus funeral rallied the people of Ireland after their defeat by the enemy; the Rossa funeral rallied the people of Ireland after the onslaught of her faithless leaders.

Will the rallied Irish people stand fast as well as he whom they honoured?

Ibid.

(Note: Terence Bellew McManus of Fermanagh died in San Francisco in 1860 at the age of 37. A Young Irelander, he was sentenced to death for High Treason by the British. That sentence was commuted to transportation for life to Van Diemans's Land. In 1852 along with Thomas Francis Meagher he escaped to the United States. The Fenian Brotherhood organised his funeral and burial in Glasnevin Cemetery, Dublin, on 10th November, 1861. Some 200,000 people are reported to have attended the funeral.)

In honouring O'Donovan Rossa the workers of Ireland are doing more than merely paying homage to an unconquerable fighter. They are signifying their adhesion to the principle of which Rossa till his latest days was a living embodiment - the principle that the freedom of a people must in the last analysis rest in the hands of that people - that there is no outside force capable of enforcing slavery upon a people really resolved to be free, and valuing freedom more than life.

O' Donovan Rossa Souvenir Book, July, 1915

The Irish Citizen Army in its constitution pledges its members to fight for a Republican Freedom for Ireland. Its members are, therefore, of the number who believe that at the call of duty they may have to lay down their lives for Ireland, and have so trained themselves that at the worst the laying down of their lives shall constitute the starting point of another glorious tradition - a tradition that will keep alive the soul of the nation.

We are, therefore, present to honour O'Donovan Rossa by right of our faith in the separate destiny of our country, and our faith in the ability of the Irish workers to achieve that destiny.

Ibid.

O'Donovan Rossa represents to us a revolutionary movement the least aristocratic and the most plebeian that ever raised itself to national dignity in Ireland. It was a movement that resting upon the masses of people in Ireland, and drawing its inspirations from the hearts of that people, was successful in inspiring its followers with such a belief in their own ability to conquer and master the future, that it nerved them to conspire for a revolt against the British Empire at a time when that empire was at peace with all the world. The mere conception of such a struggle, the stark naked fact that such a project was ever even mooted, in itself stamps as heroes all who cherished and suffered for it. Grand indeed must have been the souls, magnificent must have been the courage, splendid the idealism of the men and women who with the awful horror of the famine of Black '47, and inglorious '48, still in their minds were yet capable of rising to the spiritual level of challenging the power of England in 1865 or 1867. There were giants in those days! Are we pygmies in these?

Workers' Republic, 31st July, 1915

By the death of Comrade James Keir Hardie labour has lost one of its most fearless and incorruptible champions, and the world one of its highest minded and purest souls.

Workers' Republic, 2nd October, 1915

James Keir Hardie himself was ever too modest to say, but we who were his comrades often thought, that he was a living proof of the truth of the idea that labour could furnish in its own ranks all that was needed to achieve its own emancipation, the proof that labour needed no heaven-sent saviour from the ranks of other classes. He had been denied the ordinary chances of education, he was sent to earn his living at the age of seven, he had to educate himself in the few hours he could snatch from work, and sleep, he was blacklisted by the employers as soon as he gave vent to the voice of labour in his district, he had to face unemployment and starvation in his early manhood, and when he began to champion politically the rights of his class he found every prostitute journalist in these islands throwing mud at his character, and defaming his associates.

Ibid.

Apostles of Freedom are ever idolised when dead, but crucified when living.

Workers' Republic, 13th August, 1898

He (Wolfe Tone) was crucified in life, now he is idolised in death, and the men who push forward most arrogantly to burn incense at the altar of his fame are drawn from the very class who, were he alive today, would hasten to repudiate him as a dangerous malcontent.

Ibid.

We are told to imitate Wolfe Tone, but the greatness of Wolfe Tone lay in the fact that he imitated nobody. The needs of his time called for a man able to shake from off his mind the intellectual fetters of the past, and to unite in his own person the hopes of the new revolutionary faith and the ancient aspirations of an oppressed people; as the occasion creates the hero, so the Spirit of the Age found Wolfe Tone. And out of the seemingly unpromising material of a briefless barrister created the organising brain of an almost successful revolution, the astute diplomat, the fearless soldier, and the unconquered martyr...

Workers' Republic, 5th August, 1899

Capitalism

A striking manifestation of this fact was evinced in the action of the trade unions during the first elections under the Local Government Act of 1898. Previous to the passing of this Act the Irish workers had no vote in municipal elections, with the necessary result that local municipal government was completely in the hands of the Irish capitalist class, who kept our Irish cities pest-holes of disease and slovenliness, and made our Irish slums a horror and a byword among the cities of Europe. But in that year the aforementioned Act placed the municipal suffrage upon the same basis as the parliamentary. Immediately there sprang into existence all throughout Ireland organisations of workers aiming at wresting the municipal government from the hands of the capitalist class, and placing it in the hands of the working class. Those organisations were formed under the authority of the various Trade Councils and Land and Labour Associations, and were termed Labour Electoral Associations. They selected the constituencies, wards, to be fought solely according to the working class character of these wards, and without regard to the supposed political views of the other candidates. Loyalist and Home Ruler were equal to them; their standard was the standard of labour and under that standard the workers rallied.

The Harp, April, 1910

But with victory came demoralisation. We have said that the Irish worker was thoroughly true to his own class, but lacking in socialist knowledge. This alone offers an explanation of the subsequent set-back to the labour cause in Ireland. The men elected all over Ireland had been elected on an independent platform, and all during the election most of them had steadily refused to merge their cause in any other, and had kept their independence intact and unsullied. The splendid vote they received was the emphatic endorsement by the Irish workers of this political independence of labour. But as soon as they were elected they forgot, or seemed not to realise, this fact, and instead of forming a distinct and independent party of their own in the various councils, they allied themselves to one or other of the factions of the capitalist parties, and became labour tails of the capitalist political kites.

Ibid.

The labour party was a party only in name; it came to signify only certain men who could be trusted to draw working class support to the side of certain capitalist factions.

Ibid.

In the years immediately following that first result of the Irish workers on the field of local government the hopeless incapacity to uphold the principle of independent political action in which they had been elected, had its natural result in the overwhelming defeat of every candidate who professed to stand on a labour platform. The Irish capitalists had learned of the real weakness of the labour movement which had at first so terrified their guilty consciences, and the Irish workers had become disgusted at the poor results shown by the men they had elected. Though they were perhaps not able to frame it in so many words the Irish workers realised that a working man member of a capitalist party is not necessarily any better than a capitalist member of the same party, perhaps not so good; but that a working man who wishes to safeguard the interests of his class must withdraw from all capitalist political affiliation. And in deciding how he should vote in any great question should consult, not with the capitalist members of the Corporation, but with the committee of the organisations which secured his election.

Ibid.

Women and Freedom

What a history that would be which would tell us the history of the real women of Ireland - the women of the people! What a record of ceaseless suffering, of heroism, of martyrdom! What a recital of patient toil, of uncomplaining self-sacrifice, of unending abnegation! Aye, and what a brilliant tale of things accomplished, of deeds done, of miracles achieved!

The Harp, September, 1908

Think of all the insurrections against British tyranny in Ireland, and as you honour the men who went out to front the armed force of the oppressors think also of the brave women who kissed them and cried over them ere they went, but bade them go for freedom's sake.

Ibid.

Think of all the slimy roll of informers in Erin, and wonder when you remember how seldom even tradition places a woman's name upon the list.

Ibid.

Think of the long and bloody history of the fight against private property in Irish land - against Irish landlordism, and when you remember how the Irish mother, the woman of the house, consented to suffer eviction and ruin rather than let her husband betray the cause of his friends and neighbours, then if you believe in a God thank Him for the spirit and courage and honour of our Irish womanhood.

But then you will not be accepting princesses as the types of Irish life, you will be looking for types of the real womanhood of Ireland where only they can be found, among the producing classes.

Those Irish girls who in the recent dock strike in Belfast joined their fathers and brothers and sweethearts in the streets to battle against the English troops imported in the interests of Irish capitalism are to my mind a thousand times more admirable "types of Irish colleens" than the noblest *bean uasal* of Gaelic Erin much as I admire the latter.

Ibid.

1913-14 Industrial Strife

All the capitalist newspapers of Friday last join in urging, or giving favourable publicity to the views of others urging the employers of Dublin to join in a general lock-out of the members of the Irish Transport and General Workers' Union. It is as well. Possibly some such act is necessary in order to make that portion of the working class which still halts undecided to understand clearly what it is that lies behind the tyrannical and brow-beating attitude of the proprietors of the Dublin tramway system.

Irish Worker, 30th August, 1913

The fault of the Irish Transport and General Workers' Union! What is it? Let us tell it in plain language. Its fault is this, that it found the labourers of Ireland on their knees, and has striven to raise them to the erect position of manhood; it found them with all the vices of slavery in their souls, and it strove to eradicate these vices and replace them with some of the virtues of free men; it found them with no other weapons of defence than the arts of the liar, the lickspittle, and the toady, and it combined them and taught them to abhor those arts and rely proudly on the defensive power of combination; it, in short, found a class in whom seven centuries of social outlawry had added fresh degradations upon the burden it bore as the members of a nation suffering from the cumulative effects of seven centuries of national bondage, and out of this class, the degraded slaves of slaves more degraded still - for what degradation is more abysmal than that of those who prostitute their manhood on the altar of profit mongering? - out of this class of slaves the labourers of Dublin, the Irish Transport and General Workers' Union has created an army of intelligent self-reliant men, abhorring the old arts of the toady, the lickspittle and the crawler and trusting alone to the disciplined use of their power to labour or to withdraw their labour to assert and maintain their right as men.

Ibid.

To put it in other words, but words as pregnant with truth and meaning: the Irish Transport and General Workers' Union found that before its advent the working class of Dublin had been taught by all the educational agencies of the country, by all the social influences of their masters, that this world was created for the special benefit of the various sections of the master class, that kings and lords and capitalists were of value; that even flunkeys, toadies, lickspittle - and poodle dogs had an honoured place in the scheme of the universe, but that there was neither honour, credit, nor consideration to the man or woman who toils to maintain them all.

Ibid.

Against all this the Irish Transport and General Workers' Union has taught that they who toil are the only ones that do matter, that all others are but beggars upon the bounty of those who work with hand or brain, and that this superiority of social value can at any time be realised, be translated into actual fact, by the combination of the labouring class. Preaching, organising, and fighting upon this basis, the Irish Transport and General Workers' Union has done what? If the value of a city is to be found in the development of self-respect and high conception of social responsibilities among a people, then the Irish Transport and General Workers' Union found Dublin the poorest city in these countries by reason of its lack of these qualities. And by imbuing the workers with them, it has made Dublin the richest city in Europe today, rich by all that counts for greatness in the history of nations. It is then upon this working class so enslaved, this working class so led and so enriched with moral purposes and high aims that the employers propose to make general war.

Ibid.

I heard of one case where a labourer was asked to sign the agreement forswearing the Irish Transport and Workers' Union, and he told his employer, a small capitalist builder, that he refused to sign. The employer, knowing the man's circumstances, reminded him that he had a wife and six children who would be starving within a week. The reply of this humble labourer rose to the heights of sublimity. "It is true, sir," he said, "they will starve; but I would rather see them go out one by one in their coffins than that I should disgrace them by signing that."

And with head erect he walked out to share hunger and privation with his loved ones. Hunger and privation - and honour.

Forward, 4th October, 1913

It is a crime to deport Dublin children in order to feed, clothe and house them better than they were before. All the newspapers are against it. It is not a crime to import English scabs to take the bread out of the mouth of Dublin men, women and children, and reduce them to slavery.

The newspapers are overjoyed about it. Fellow-workers! All the collection of hyprocrites and sweaters who paraded our docks and railway stations a few days ago, and prostituted the name of religion to suit the base ends of those who for generations have grown fat by grinding the faces of the poor, are silent as the grave in the face of the importation of British scabs. They poured insult, lies and calumny upon the British labour men and women who offered our children the shelter and comfort of their homes in the day of our trial; but they allow British blacklegs to enter Dublin without a word of protest!

Irish Worker, 8th November, 1913

During the progress of the present dispute we have seen imported into Dublin some of the lowest elements from the very dregs of the criminal population of Great Britain and Ireland. This scum of the underworld have come here excited by appeals to the vilest instincts of their natures, these appeals being framed and made by the gentlemen employers of Dublin. They have been incited to betray their fellows fighting against the imposition of an agreement denounced by the highest Court of Inquiry, as well as by public opinion in general, as an interference with individual liberty. And in order to induce them to act as Judases their rascally passions were pandered to by the offer of wages higher than were ever paid to union men, and by the permission and encouragement to carry murderous weapons. Too much stress cannot be laid upon this latter encouragement. There are natures so low that permission to carry about the means whereby life may be destroyed has to them an irresistible appeal; the feeling that they carry in their pockets the possibility of destroying others, has to these base natures an intoxication all its own. To that feeling the employers of Dublin deliberately appealed. Deliberately, and with malice aforethought, they armed a gang of the lowest scoundrels in these islands, and after daily inflaming them with drink, sent them to and fro in the streets of the capital, inciting and maddening all those whose liberties they were helping to make war. In one of the streets on Thursday afternoon, this cold-blooded policy of incitement to outrage had its effect. A few men jeered at the passing scabs and made a show of hostility. Immediately a scab drew a revolver, fired - and shot one of the employers principally responsible for bringing him here and principally responsible for arming him and setting him loose primed with drink upon the streets of Dublin. That action of the employer in importing and arming such a scoundrel was a crime - an anti-social crime of the foulest nature - and surely never more dramatically did a crime bring its own punishment. It came like a judgement from on high, and what wonder if such was the first thought of the workers when the news was told!

Irish Worker, 13th December, 1913

I have always told our friends in Great Britain that our fight in Ireland was neither inspired nor swayed by theories nor theorists. It grew and was hammered out of the hard necessities of our situation. Here, in this brief synopsis, you can trace its growth for yourselves. First a fierce desire to save our brothers of the sea, a desire leading to us risking our own existence in their cause. Developing from that an extension of the principle of sympathetic action until we took the fierce beast of capital by the throat all over Dublin, and loosened its hold on the vitals of thousands of our class. Then a rally of the forces of capital to recover their hold, and eventually a titanic struggle, in which the forces of labour in Britain openly, and the forces of capital secretly, became participants.

Daily Herald, 6th December, 1913

Publicists of all kinds, philanthropists, literary men, lovers of their kind, poets, brilliant writers, artists, have all been conquered by the valiant heroism of the Dublin workers, have all been drawn within the ranks of the friends of the fighters of labour - all have succumbed to the magic charm of the unobtrusive men and women whose constancy amidst sufferings has made this fight possible.

Irish Worker, 20th December, 1913

The dramatic suddenness with which the Dublin fight was thrust upon public attention, the tragic occurrences of the first few days - working class martyrdom, the happy coincidence of a Trade Union Congress, the intervention of British trade unionists to assert the right of public meeting for Irish workers - filling the gap in the ranks caused by the jailing of Irish Trade Union leaders, the brilliant inspiration of a food ship, and last but not least the splendid heroism of the Dublin men and women showing out against the background of the squalor and misery of their houses.

Forward, 9th February, 1914

And now? Dublin is isolated. We asked our friends of the transport trade unions to isolate the capitalist class of Dublin, and we asked the other unions to back them up. But no, they said we would rather help you by giving you funds. We argued that a strike is an attempt to stop the capitalist from carrying on his business, that the success or failure of the strike depends entirely upon the success or non-success of the capitalist to do without the strikers. If the capitalist is able to carry on his business without the strikers, then the strike is lost, even if the strikers receive more in strike pay than they formerly did in wages. We said that if scabs are working a ship and union men discharge in another port the boat so loaded, then those union men are strike breakers, since they help the capitalist in question to carry on his business. That if union seamen man a boat discharged by scabs, these union seamen or firemen are by the same reason strike-breakers as also are the railwaymen or carters who assist in transporting the goods handled by the scabs for the capitalist who is fighting his men or women. In other words, we appealed to the collective soul of the workers against the collective hatred of the capitalist.

Ibid.

But why go on? Sufficient to say that the working class unity of the first days of the Dublin fight was sacrificed in the interests of sectional officialism. The officials failed to grasp the opportunity offered to them to make a permanent reality of the unions of working class forces brought into being by the spectacle of rebellion, martyrdom and misery exhibited by the workers of Dublin. All England and Scotland rose to it; working class officialdom and working class rank and file alike responded to the call of inspiration; it would have raised us all upward and onward towards our common emancipation. But sectionalism, intrigues and old-time jealousies damned us in the hour of victory, and officialdom was the first to fall to the tempter.

And so we Irish workers must go down into Hell, bow our backs to the lash of the slave driver, let our hearts be seared by the iron of his hatred, and instead of the sacramental wafer of brotherhood and common sacrifice, eat the dust of defeat and betrayal.

Ibid.

General

During a lock-out in Dundalk at the beginning of last year, a girl picket was arrested for striving to induce another girl not to blackleg. She was summarily tried and sentenced to prison on a charge of "indecent conduct in the streets". No unclean language or action had been attributed to her and the police evidence simply stated that she had persisted in picketing, yet the cold-blooded scoundrelism of the authorities framed a charge against her calculated to blast her character and ruin her whole life. If she had been a daughter of an Irish farmer fighting an Irish landlord in Land League days the then Irish Party would have made the world ring with their denunciations of such character assassinations; but she was only an Irish working girl fighting an Irish employer, and none of the Irish heroes who, on the platforms of the Liberal Party in England, are fighting for the "Glory of God and the Honour of Erin", had time to waste on such as her.

Forward, 3rd May, 1913

Should the working class of Europe, rather than slaughter each other for the benefit of kings and financiers, proceed tomorrow to erect barricades all over Europe, to break up bridges and destroy the transport service that war might be abolished, we should be perfectly justified in following such a glorious example and contributing our aid to the final dethronement of the vulture classes that rule and rob the world.

Irish Worker, 8th August, 1914

We acknowledge no right in another individual or class to withhold anything which is ours by right of labour. We are out for justice and we have assailed or contested no just liberty. We know our duties as we know our rights and we shall stand by one another through thick and thin prepared, if necessary, to arm and achieve by force our place in the world, and also to maintain it by force. These be the ends of our fight - and should the heavens fall we shall achieve them.

Irish Worker, 25th October, 1913

Irish Citizen Army

The Irish Citizen Army was founded during the great Dublin Lock-Out of 1913-14, for the purpose of protecting the working class, and of preserving its right of public meeting and free association. The streets of Dublin had been covered by the bodies of helpless men, women, boys and girls brutally batoned by the uniformed bullies of the British Government.

Three men had been killed, and one young Irish girl murdered by a scab, and nothing was done to bring the assassins to justice. So since justice did not exist for us, since the law instead of protecting the rights of the workers was an open enemy, and since the armed forces of the Crown were unreservedly at the disposal of the enemies of labour, it was resolved to create our own army to secure our rights, to protect our members, and to be a guarantee of our own free progress.

Workers' Republic, 30th October, 1915

An armed organisation of the Irish working class is a phenomenon in Ireland. Hitherto the workers of Ireland have fought as parts of the armies led by their masters, never as members of an army officered, trained, and inspired by men of their own class. Now, with arms in their hands, they propose to steer their own course, to carve their own future.

Neither Home Rule, nor the lack of Home Rule, will make them lay down their arms.

Ibid.

However it may be for others, for us of the Citizen Army there is but one ideal - an Ireland ruled, and owned by Irish men and women, sovereign and independent from the centre to the sea, and flying its own flag outward over all the oceans.

We cannot be swerved from our course by honeyed words, lulled into carelessness by freedom to parade and strut in uniforms, nor betrayed by high-sounding phrases.

The Irish Citizen Army will only co-operate in a forward movement. The moment that forward movement ceases it reserves to itself the right to step out of the alignment, and advance by itself if needs be, in an effort to plant the banner of freedom one reach further towards its goal ...

Ibid.

James Connolly's Last Statement

at

The Field General Court Martial
at Dublin Castle, 9th May, 1916

I do not wish to make any defence except against charges of wanton cruelty to prisoners. These trifling allegations that have been made, if they record facts that really happened, deal only with the almost unavoidable incidents of a hurried uprising against long established authority, and nowhere show evidence of set purpose to wantonly injure unarmed persons.

We went out to break the connection between this country and the British Empire, and to establish an Irish Republic. We believed that the call we then issued to the people of Ireland, was a nobler call, in a holier cause, than any call issued to them during this war, having any connection with the war. We succeeded in proving that Irishmen are ready to die endeavouring to win for Ireland those national rights which the British Government has been asking them to die to win for Belgium. As long as that remains the case, the cause of Irish freedom is safe. Believing that the British Government has no right in Ireland, never had any right in Ireland, and never can have any right in Ireland, the presence in any one generation of Irishmen of even a respectable minority ready to die to affirm that truth, makes that Government for ever a usurpation and a crime against human progress. I personally thank God that I have lived to see the day when thousands of Irish men and boys, and hundreds of Irish women and girls, were ready to affirm that truth, and to attest it with their lives if need be.

James Connolly
Commandant-General, Dublin Division,
Army of the Irish Republic

Biographical Chronology

James Connolly
5 June 1868 - 12 May 1916

1868   Born at 107, Cowgate, Edinburgh, on 5 June, son of John Connolly, lamplighter, and Mary McGinn. John Connolly was born in Ireland and was an Irish speaker. Mary McGinn was born in Monaghan, Ireland.

1882   Joined the Royal Scots Regiment of the British Army. Arrived at Cork, Ireland, with this Regiment in July 1882. Served in Ireland until February 1889.

1889   John Connolly had an accident which fitted him for light work only. James left the Army four months before he was due to be discharged. Joined the Social-Democratic Federation in Dundee, Scotland.

1890   Married Lillie Reynolds, a Wicklow Protestant, one of whose ancestors was hanged as a rebel in 1798.

1893   Correspondent for *Justice*, Scottish socialist journal.

1894   Working as a cobbler.

1895   Socialist candidate in local authority election in Edinburgh. Itinerant lecturer on socialist matters.

1896   James Connolly appointed organiser of Dublin Socialist Club. Together with seven other Dublin-based workers formed the Irish Socialist Republican Party on 29 May 1896.

1897 Founded the 'Rank and File '98 Club' to spread knowledge of the aims of the United Irishmen. Joined with Maud Gonne, John O'Leary, W.B. Yeats and others to organise and participate in demonstrations against the celebrations of Queen Victoria's Jubilee. Arrested after police baton charge.

1898 Founded *Workers' Republic*, a weekly journal in support of democracy, a Republic for Ireland, and the abolition of landlordism.

1899 Leader of the campaign against the British war on the Boers. Succeeded in reducing recruitment for the British Army to a minimum.

1901 Speaking tour in Britain. Elected to Dublin Trades Council by the United Labourers' Union. Stood as Labour Candidate in Wood Quay Ward for Dublin Corporation. Victim of slander campaign by priests and publicans. Priests preached that he was an Anti-Christ and those who voted for him risked excommunication. Invited to become Secretary of the Builders' Labourers' Union but declined.

1902 Took part in socialist conferences in Scotland. Left for a speaking tour of the United States, under the auspices of the American Socialist Labour Party.

1903 Socialist candidate in Wood Quay Ward, Dublin. Connolly family emigrated to the U.S. Accidental death of eldest daughter, Mona, in Dublin.

1903-10 Active in socialist and trades union movement in the U.S. Organiser for Industrial Workers of the World. Involved in Irish-American revolutionary affairs. Founded *The Harp*, a socialist Irish journal in the U.S.

1910 Published *Labour, Nationality and Religion*, and his classic work *Labour in Irish History* which established him as a socialist thinker, teacher and historian. Joined the Irish Transport Workers' Union. In Belfast as an organiser for that union.

1912 At Trade Union conference in Clonmel supported a resolution to establish an independent Labour Party for Ireland. Party not then formed owing to lukewarm attitude towards it of James Larkin and the general lack of enthusiasm of trades union officials. Socialist candidate in Dock Ward for Belfast City Council.

1913-14 Took leading part in the labour industrial struggle in Dublin. A founder of the Irish Citizen Army. Addressed mass rallies at Beresford Place in Dublin.

1914 Agitated against proposals to establish an Orange State in Ulster. Irish T.U.C. became 'Irish T.U.C. and Labour Party' on 1 June with Connolly's backing. Connolly elected to National Executive Council. Backed women's suffrage. On outbreak of Great War in August declared that workers should not participate in it and that recruiting for the British Army in Ireland should be resisted. Began regular association with Thomas J. Clarke, Patrick H. Pearse, Seán Mac Diarmada, Seán T. Ó Ceallaigh, Arthur Griffith, Eamonn Ceannt, Major John MacBride, Thomas MacDonagh and the Countess Markievicz and started preparations for organising an insurrection during the course of the War.

James Connolly, chosen as President of the Irish Neutrality League with Seán T. Ó Ceallaigh as Secretary and Thomas Farren as Treasurer. The Committee consisted of the Countess Markievicz, Francis Sheehy-Skeffington, Arthur Griffith, Seán Milroy, J.J. Scollan and William O'Brien.

Following departure of James Larkin to America, Connolly became acting-General Secretary of the Irish Transport Workers' Union and Editor of *Irish Worker* which he turned into a revolutionary paper.

1915 Organisational work for Union, writing revolutionary and socialist articles and speaking at public meetings against the War. Reorganised Irish Citizen Army as a potential revolutionary republican fighting force. Became aware of plans for insurrection by Military Council of the Irish Republican Brotherhood. Involved himself and the I.C.A. in these preparations.

1916   Arrangements made for a general uprising against British rule to take place on Easter Sunday 23 April at 6.30 p.m. Open parades of Irish Volunteers and Irish Citizen Army on St. Patrick's Day. Connolly's play 'Under Which Flag' produced at Liberty Hall. Orders for a general rising were countermanded by the Irish Volunteer Chief of Staff, Professor Eoin Mac Neill, who was opposed to insurrection. As a result, the Rising was confirmed to Dublin, Galway, Wexford and Louth. James Connolly, a signatory of the Proclamation of the Irish Republic, was Commander-in- Chief of Republican forces in Dublin. He was wounded twice during the week-long fighting. After the surrender James Connolly was tried by British Court Martial and sentenced to death. Together with Seán Mac Diarmada, he was executed on 12 May.